# 50 and F*ck It!

## Martina E. Faulkner, LMSW

INSPIREBYTES OMNI MEDIA

**50 and F\*ck It!** *Learn How You Can Let Go, Stand In Your Boots, and Truly Live!*

This publication is distributed worldwide in the English language in the following formats:

ISBN Hardcover: 978-1-953445-30-8
ISBN Paperback: 978-1-953445-28-5
ISBN E-Book: 978-1-953445-29-2

Library of Congress Control Number: 2022945269

This book was responsibly printed using print-on-demand technology, in order to minimize its impact on the planet and the environment. Learn more at: www.inspirebytes.com/why-we-publish-differently/

 INSPIREBYTES OMNI MEDIA

Inspirebytes Omni Media LLC
PO Box 988
Wilmette, IL 60091

For more information, please visit www.inspirebytes.com

*Author photos © SpiderMeka Portraits*
*Interior Illustrations © Frances E. Vail*

*To all my friends, all along the way,*

*May we truly know what it means to
live in joy, love, and peace—
and especially to my high school crew for
being some of the best, most amazing women
I have the privilege and pleasure of knowing.*

# Contents

# Introduction

2022 is the year I turned 50. My birthday is in February, so it was also the end of the 24th month of the Covid-19 pandemic as well as the end of my third year as a small business owner. For me, 2022 represented both the end of some very challenging years and the start of a brand new decade.

I don't know about you, but when I was younger, 50 felt old. Like, *really* old. Back then, I remember hearing about people retiring or even dying in their 50s, and here I am just getting started.

As a result, I gravitate toward the stories of people who reinvented (or found) themselves later in life, or who managed to achieve their "breakthrough" sometime after 50. These stories buoy me when it all feels like too much. They remind me that age is just a number you count along the way, and it's *how you choose* to count that number that matters.

These reflections led me to create a massive shift in my thinking in the months before my birthday. I knew I didn't want to continue living life the way I always had. In fact, over the past two decades, I had been diligently transforming my life into something that was more meaningful and aligned than ever before. But still, this birthday—this milestone—loomed large in my mind. For me, it represented a line in the sand. I could choose to keep going as I always had, slowly but deliberately chipping away at change—or I could choose something different.

I chose something different.

And then the Universe gave me an early birthday gift.

About two weeks before my birthday, I got an unsolicited email from a troll via my website. Now, my website is set up so that you have to jump through a few hoops to send me an email. So this showed me that the person really made an effort to share his thoughts with me in an unkind way. In the past, I probably would have given it some air time, but this time, I looked at it and said, "Fuck it!" Then I promptly deleted it and updated the settings on my website. Since I was no longer taking new clients, there was no need to have an online form to reach me.

That single act was like a spark that ignited my entire attitude toward life after 50. "Fuck it!" quickly became the motto I would use to shift everything around me. I would welcome this milestone year in a different way, instead of the more demure "50 and Fabulous" or aspirational "Fit by 50," as so many of my other friends have shared.

No, for me it's: 50 and Fuck It!

It has a freedom to it that is empowering beyond anything I could have imagined.

Of course, as with everything any author writes, this book is based on my own experience, witnessing, and knowledge. This means that you might get to a chapter and think, *This doesn't apply to me; my experience is different.* Yes. It's highly likely, actually. All of our lived experiences are different in the details. However, it's where the overlap occurs that we can connect and share in our common humanity. That's where the gold is.

Based on some early feedback, this may especially be true for the chapter on menopause. While I reached out to friends in their late 50s and early 60s for some examples of what could happen during menopause (since I'm just at the beginning), it's by no means certain that what I wrote will happen to you. Maybe you won't experience hot flashes, but you might feel cold all the time. Or perhaps you won't have any symptoms at all and just breeze through the transition—I know I'm hoping for that. It's all good. It's all okay. And it's all valid, and that's the point.

The point of this entire book is to help you reclaim (or discover) your unique attitude and perspective on your own life—which includes anything that's different from what I've shared here. The goal is to empower you to *be who you are* and live fully from there.

Of course, "fuck it" can have connotations of "not giving a fuck", which is akin to not caring or caring less, being aloof, or even being unkind. But that's not what this is. Fuck It! is not about *not* caring or caring less. It's about caring *more*—more deeply, more passionately, and more deliberately. It's about focusing on the things that really matter to you and letting the rest fall away. This means you consciously choose to focus on *your* life, *your* time, *your* values, and *your whole self,* and then make decisions from there in alignment with who you are.

That's where Fuck It! is both liberating and empowering at the same time. This is about standing in your boots, being who you are, and claiming your place in the world... from a place of deep caring and connection to yourself.

To that end, I have drafted a Fuck It! Manifesto and Proclamation to clearly share the sentiment behind the phrase and the meaning behind its use. I hope it brings you as much freedom, joy, and laughter(!) as it has brought me.

You're 50 now, so welcome to your new Fuck It! Life.

## The Fuck It! Manifesto

Fuck It! isn't mean.

Fuck It! isn't cruel.

Fuck It! isn't the same as "fuck you!" or "fuck off!"

Fuck It! isn't about putting others down, bullying, or shaming anyone.

Fuck It! isn't about imposing your will or beliefs on others.

Fuck It! is about standing in your boots and claiming your place on this great rock of ours, spinning through space.

Fuck It! is about owning who you are at this moment in time—boldly and proudly going forward with the mentality that you are 100% worth it.

Fuck It! is about being able to be exactly who you are and choose how you're going to go about living your life.

Fuck It! is about embracing life and embracing yourself in whatever way is best for you.

## The Fuck It! Proclamation

I am who I am, and who I am is exactly who I am meant to be.

I will not apologize for being my best self.

I will no longer say yes to things that don't align with who I am deep inside.

I choose to honor myself and prioritize my needs and values.

I choose me.

Fuck It! is both freeing and freedom. With boundaries, communication, and managed expectations—and a playful wink in your heart—you can fully embrace the Fuck It! Lifestyle and truly live!

# Chapter 1

# You Do You, Boo

"You do you, boo" is a phrase I have never uttered in my life. Until now.

I *have* said "you do you" many times over. It's a phrase that's common among wellness professionals. I've also used "Boo" as a nickname for my niece. When she was just six months old, I played peek-a-boo with her, and it stuck. I've never combined them, though, and actually uttered, "You do you, boo," until writing this book. I'm not hip enough for it. Seriously. But I like a good rhyme, so for the purpose of this book, it works.

What doesn't work perfectly, however, is the sentiment of empowerment expressed through the lens of permission inherent in the phrase. (That was a lot of words.)

Basically, I have a love/hate relationship with the idea of giving someone else permission, unless it's a child. Then I think permission is a good tool to teach boundaries in order for children to have something to push against to develop properly. But I digress.

Fortunately or unfortunately, in our world (especially in the wellness industry), we have adopted this idea of "permission" as a means of empowerment. On the surface, this sounds good. But scratch a little, and it starts to fall apart.

Empowerment is great. Permission is less great.

Permission implies that someone else is in control. Yes, even if you're giving it to yourself. Because if you are, then that means you're still agreeing with some sort of external expectation, and that's where it becomes a problem.

Permission actually limits empowerment.

Now, being empowered and modeling a behavior for someone else is not the same as giving them permission, though it's often framed that way. If being yourself *inspires* someone else to do the same, that's magical. If being yourself gives someone else *permission* to do the same, then their authenticity is tied to—or dependent on—someone else. In this example, that someone else is you. Yikes!

So let's look at "you do you, boo" as less of a permission slip and more of a motto, something to reinforce what's already within us: a longing for authenticity and being who we are.

## Apology *not* accepted

I have a friend who is also an author and writer. Years ago, she introduced me to the phrase "unapologetically myself"—which is her tagline. Her name is Carla Birnberg, and she lives life out loud on her terms. It's not neat and tidy. It's not tied up with a bow in pretty packaging. It's real. It's raw. It's messy. And it's all hers. As a result, it's absolutely magical to be friends with her. On a regular basis, she shares her humanity through her wins and and her challenges, and she does it with humor, passion, and love.

Carla's ability to live an unapologetic life is a model that has inspired me time and time again. When she gets something wrong, she may apologize for her behavior or decision, but she never apologizes for being herself. And that's the main difference between being unapologetically yourself and living a life constantly apologizing for simply being alive.

When you apologize for just being on the planet, you are essentially saying that you shouldn't count as a human being. Unfortunately, I've done this in the past, and I know many other people (mostly women) who have done it, too. It's almost as if we've been trained to apologize for existing... unless we meet certain criteria deemed worthy enough of breathing and taking up space and oxygen. But again, I digress.

Here's what I know about apologizing:

Most of the time, when someone says they're sorry, they're not actually apologizing. It's a reflexive statement that pops easily out of our mouths. When you actually pause long enough to ask what they're sorry about, they don't always have an answer. So "I'm sorry" as a phrase needs to be reserved for the times we are *actually* apologizing for something. How different our lives would be if we simply stopped apologizing for anything and everything and allowed ourselves to to take up space. We have to start somewhere, so let's start there.

Remove "I'm sorry" from your life (unless you are actually apologizing) and see what happens. After that, you can start to reclaim who you are. At 50, it's not too late. It's never too late (or too early).

## An invitation

This book is about many things, but at its core, it's about standing in your boots, being who you are, and claiming your place in the world. Not obnoxiously (that's equivalent to "fuck you!" or "fuck off!") or apologetically (that's equivalent to "fuck me"), but sincerely with a calm inner strength and sense of self.

When I say "you do you, boo," it's an invitation to be who you are from that deep, internal place. To pull on your unique pair of boots and stand up. Some of us (or many of us) might have to fall a few times before we get our footing (I most certainly did), and that's okay. What matters is that you're not standing in someone else's boots—or stealing someone else's boots—to do it.

Think about wearing someone else's shoes or boots. It's uncomfortable, right? The heel height might be wrong, or the width or length might be off, even if you wear the same size. Someone else's well-worn shoes will never fit you properly. You have to wear your own, break them in, and make them yours.

"You do you, boo" is an invitation to do just that. It's an invitation to empowerment, made with love. I've walked this path myself. I know how much love and support it takes to stand up. I also know that it takes even more to stand up *after* falling down. Paulo Coelho (one of my favorite authors) wrote: "The secret of life, though, is to fall seven times and get up eight times." *(The Alchemist)*

We all fall down. All of us. You will fall, especially if you've been wearing someone else's boots for a while and you're putting your own boots on for the first time. Just like all new shoes need a bit of breaking in, your boots will, too.

You'll fall, you'll get blisters, you may need orthotics, but the secret lies in knowing that for the first time, you're facing life on your own terms, in your own boots, without apologizing. And that's fucking magical!

For the rest of the book, I'm going to share the various ways I have figured out how to live the Fuck It! Lifestyle... from tangible tips to personal anecdotes to inspirational ideas.

Turning 50 made me feel unshackled. It gave me breath in a way that made me realize I had been barely breathing, or shallow breathing at best. It was the milestone moment that I chose to use to transform how I go from here. And just like with everything else, it's not binary. It's not an "all or nothing" or "black and white" endeavor. It's a spectrum of progress and behavior that is now fueled by a different thought. For much of my younger life, a lot of my thoughts or beliefs were grounded in the Land of Should. "Should" is living in the binary world of black and white expressed through an uninspirational spectrum of grey, instead of embracing life for the wondrous technicolor it is—or can be.

I *should* do this. I *should* say that. I *should* be more (or less).

If you've read any self-help books, this concept won't be new to you. Heck, I stopped using the word "should" almost two decades ago when I first learned about it. But *using* it and *thinking* it are two very different things.

Even if you've stopped saying "should" and raised your awareness to its use in your life, my guess is that somewhere deep down, you may still *think* it. It's much harder to change a pattern of thought than a pattern of behavior. You still have beliefs or thoughts that creep in and suggest to you how something should be. Including how others *should* be—or how *you* should be. "Should" is disempowering. It instantly takes you out of your boots and away from yourself.

Once you start listening to the shoulds in your head, everything else gets drowned out. It's as if "should" is a white noise keeping you stuck on that good old hamster wheel of externalized happiness—making you deaf to your own voice.

One thing I've learned from going through this process is this: When I stopped caring what others thought, I could suddenly hear my own voice. And I listened.

So with every chapter, there is an inherent invitation. The invitation is simple: *Listen to your own voice.* Take what I've shared and look at your own life. Apply it if it helps, ignore if it doesn't. What I've written here is meant to inspire you to *be who you are.* To be your best self, your true self. I'll be over here being me in the best ways I can, and I invite you to be you. Magical, brilliant, wondrous you. It's time.

Fuck It!—it's time for you to do you, boo.

## Chapter 2

# Celebrate Yourself

On my 50th birthday, I celebrated in all the ways we typically celebrate birthdays. I had dinner with dear friends and family, I chatted on the phone with people near and far, and I received countless texts, cards, and other messages of love and celebration. I also did something I've never done before: I celebrated myself.

The day before my birthday, I baked my favorite cake (classic yellow butter cake with chocolate fudge frosting—yum!). I knew my mom had bought me a cake that would probably be delicious (I mean, who doesn't love cake?), but I wanted my *favorite* cake on my birthday, especially as it was my 50th.

In the past, I would have simply had the cake my mom got instead of baking my own and said something to myself like:

*"Don't upset anyone."*

*"Be grateful for the cake, even if it's not your favorite."*

*"It's just cake. Why do you care so much? What's wrong with you?"*

*"You're not supposed to bake your own cake on your birthday."*

*"If you bake your own cake, you're kind of a jerk."*

All of these thoughts are often followed by a whole bunch of other thoughts from the Land of Should, such as:

*"Someone else should be making a cake for you."*

*"You shouldn't have to make your own cake."*

*"What is everyone else going to think about you? You should worry about that."*

*"What is everyone else going to think about themselves if you do this? You really should worry about that!"*

But on this occasion, I said, "Fuck It!" instead. I went to the store and bought the ingredients to bake my favorite cake. It wasn't about anybody else (remember the Fuck It! Manifesto). This was about me honoring myself, standing in my boots, and claiming what would make me happy—and then going and doing it.

And let me tell you, that cake was awesome!

In our family, we have a tradition of waking the birthday person up early (as a kid it was often 6 a.m. or earlier) by singing *Happy Birthday* and starting the day with cake and presents. If you don't have this tradition, I highly recommend it, especially if you have kids. For starters, what kid doesn't want to have cake for breakfast? For that matter, what adult wouldn't be equally as excited about it? Cake for breakfast is always a fun option. (In fact, I maintain that adults invented muffins in order to sneakily have cake for breakfast. Think about it...)

Anyway, as a kid, getting to open your presents first thing in the morning and then enjoying them all day *on the day of your birthday* is pretty awesome. It makes the day special in a way that nothing else can, and it really starts your birthday on a happy note.

So after waking up to my favorite cake, a cup of hot tea, and a pile of presents from friends and family, I set about my day. The difference this time was that I *chose* to let people know it was my birthday. I had a relatively full schedule of appointments that included: physical therapy, a haircut, and two MRIs (yes, it was the only day they could schedule me within a month's time). To all of these appointments, I proudly wore a "Happy Birthday" headband.

Everywhere I went, people greeted me with a smile and a "Happy Birthday!" Complete strangers came up to me to wish me well, and the people I knew smiled and laughed with me and said things like: "You're too funny!" "That's so cool!" and "I need one of those!"

There's something infectious about a person showing up in life, happily being who they are without apology or shame, and enjoying themselves. Not at the expense of anyone else, and not in a boastful, obnoxious way (remember, those are "Fuck you!" attitudes). On that day, I was that person, and I could see the ripple effects of something as simple as wearing a festive headband that declared it was my birthday. I said "thank you" every time, and my smile just grew and grew throughout the day.

Interestingly, I could also see the discomfort it gave some people to see someone else so comfortable in their boots. I could see a couple people grimace at the display of joy in front of them. I don't know if that's because of me showing up like that or because they were already having a bad day. I'm not here to take someone else's inventory. It's just something I noticed and wondered about, but it never stopped me from feeling joyful.

So my crown and I spent the day together, in and out of appointments, happily celebrating the fact that my parents had sex, and I was born. My self-celebration was a seemingly small gesture that had significance well beyond its tangible scope.

The thing is, we rarely celebrate ourselves. If we do, it can be looked at as boastful or narcissistic. But in my opinion, if we don't, that's worse. By not celebrating ourselves, we 1) leave it to everyone else around us to celebrate us, and 2) we send a signal to ourselves that we're not worthy of being celebrated.

In the first instance, we open ourselves up to all kinds of disappointment because being celebrated by others requires good communication skills combined with good expectation management. I can't tell you the number of clients and friends I've spoken with over the years who shared stories of disappointment because someone in their life got it wrong. Yes, "it's the thought that counts," but it's also more than that. If your partner of 20 years buys you something that makes you feel unseen, unheard, or unknown, it hurts. It's that simple.

In the second instance, we run the risk of reinforcing negative belief systems or thought patterns that started out externalized and over time became internalized, with the basic sentiment being that we are not enough just as we are. Again, if you've read any self-help books, you know this theme. But it's hard to actually feel like you're enough if you're not willing to (or feel scared to) have your own back. If you think about it like this, it might make more sense:

If your best friend were having a birthday, what would you do? Would you pretend like it wasn't happening? Or would you take the opportunity to celebrate them? My guess is you'd do the latter, so why not do it for yourself?

Ultimately, we teach people how to treat us by how we treat ourselves. If you always put yourself last, you're showing others that it's okay for them to put you last, too. This is more than "put your oxygen mask on first" (though that's a good metaphor); this is about knowing that you're *deserving* of putting your oxygen mask on first. It's about changing the genesis thoughts behind the actions, and you do that by celebrating yourself!

## Make it fun!

Many self-help books feel rather serious sometimes, don't they? If there's one thing I've learned, it's that people learn better when they're having fun. So make it fun! My birthday headband could just as easily have been a tiara, a crown, a pin/button, a hat, a tee-shirt, or anything else. There's a reason why tee-shirts that say "Kiss me, I'm Irish" sell well around St. Patrick's Day. They're a bit cheeky and fun. My birthday headband was made of red velvet and had five velvet candles standing upright three to four inches above my head with one more candle flopping on either side of the five. It had gold tinsel on it, and the candles came in every color. It also had a sign on the front that read "Happy Birthday!" It was shiny, colorful, and unmistakable. You couldn't miss it. And it was a lot of fun! (See my pic in the back of the book!)

I kept it on throughout the day all the way through dinner at a fancy-ish local restaurant. I figured if I was going to celebrate my birthday, I would do it out loud. I wasn't disappointed. This was my best birthday yet, for many reasons, one of which was simply the fact that I was celebrating myself alongside everybody else in my life. It made everything sweeter, brighter, and happier. I was in a truly festive mood on my birthday, which ended up lasting for a few days and included the aforementioned favorite cake!

I had a slice every morning for breakfast for four days in a row. It was delicious, and I savored every single bite. I didn't make it transactional, either. There was no exchange of one thing for another. That's not what celebrating yourself is about. There's no "if this, then that" when it comes to being your own best friend and champion. That's an old way of thinking. You don't have to "earn" your own attention, praise, or celebration.

So I didn't "allow" myself cake by doing something else. I simply had cake. And I enjoyed it. Every day. Until I didn't want cake anymore. Until it didn't feel celebratory. I had cake while it was fun, and I stopped having cake when it wasn't fun. (Yes, there was still cake left on day four, and we threw out what was left.)

## Milestones are actually benches

In addition to birthdays, it's important to celebrate ourselves when it comes to achievements or milestones. These are the benches on the paths of our lives that give it punctuated meaning. They invite us to sit down, pause, and look around, hopefully so we can savor the moment—or at the very least, honor it. One of the things I tell my fellow authors when their first book is coming out is to celebrate and savor it. All of it. Every text, every message, every email, every phone call, every comment. Savor it and celebrate it. You only get a few "firsts" in life, and if you don't celebrate them, who will? This reminds me of the quote by Byron Katie: "It's not your job to like me—it's mine." I'd say the same goes for celebrating ourselves. It's not someone else's job to celebrate you, it's yours. If someone else *does* celebrate you, consider that a bonus or a gift. First and foremost, however, celebrate yourself. It's important.

When I published my first book, I went all out. I hosted my own cocktail party, gave a speech, read an excerpt, and got to spend a few hours visiting with friends and family, enjoying everything. I celebrated myself and my achievement. It was one of the best events of my life because I was able to stand in my boots and say "I'm an author" to the people who knew me best, and have them in return say "Congratulations!" It was a big deal, and it still is a big deal, so much so that I started a tradition with that first book.

Every time I publish another book, I have a small charm made by a jeweler in California. The charms are simple silver "dog tags" hand-stamped with the initials of my book titles and the year. I now have a necklace with five such charms on it, and it continues to grow. Each book is a milestone marker in my life, and being able to look back on them all through something tangible is really special.

Of course, events in your life don't have to be "big" to count. It's just as important to mark the milestones that have meaning to you but may seem less important, or smaller, to the onlooker.

I remember the first time I could move my toe again after more than three years of immobility due to an injury. When I was able to wiggle it just a few weeks after the surgery, I almost cried. My surgeon got a huge smile on his face because he knew this was a game changer for me. It meant I could walk around the block again. The block is a simple ¾ mile that I had not been able to complete for at least a year by the time I had surgery on my foot. My doctor and I both knew this was a milestone for me. The new nurse in the room, however, looked confused. She had never met me, and she had a look that seemed to say, "It's just a toe, he fixes them for a living. What's the big deal?"

I didn't need her to know. I knew, and that was enough. The fact that my doctor also knew made it a little bit more meaningful. I celebrated that afternoon. How? I walked to my car, put on music, opened my windows, and drove with the sun and a smile on my face. I drove and sang along with the music until I got to a point where the emotion hit me so hard that I just parked and cried. Happy, happy tears. Tears of relief, tears of gratitude, tears of joy. I knew I would be able to walk properly again, even though I also knew it would take some time to get there. In my mind, that was more than enough reason to celebrate.

Every milestone, no matter how big or small, is an opportunity to celebrate yourself. Some people scrapbook while some people frame things and hang them on the wall (I'm in the second group). Other people make photo books or write in their journals. Some throw parties while others announce it on social media. I have done all of these and more.

When I was getting a divorce, I made a wall of "me" photos. I did this to remind myself just how happy I can be and how awesome my life has been overall. Each photo contained a picture of me. Some were smiling, some were more serious, and all of them were photos of me *being me*. It was one of the best gifts I ever gave myself. I woke up every morning and went to bed every night seeing a wall of photos that reminded me to celebrate myself, that reminded me that I would be okay, and that I mattered and could take up space.

I believe in celebrating myself, my life, and my accomplishments, just as I believe in doing the same for my friends. Because I am my own friend.

That is the single greatest shift that can come from celebrating yourself: Seeing yourself as—and knowing you are—your own best friend.

So say "Fuck It!" and celebrate yourself. However, whenever, and for whatever reason you want. I can't recommend it enough.

## Chapter 3

# No Tagging Allowed

Do you know what "tagging" is? I ask because I didn't. Apparently it's when someone graffitis a wall. Technically, it's "the repeated use of a single symbol or series of symbols to mark territory." (I got that from Britannica.com. Who else grew up with a set of the Encyclopedia Britannica in their house? We even had a dedicated bookcase for ours!)

Anyway, tagging. How did I learn the term and why does it matter when you're 50? Let's go back to the troll who emailed me a couple weeks before my birthday...

After I deleted his email and changed my email settings, I felt empowered. I felt ready to take more control of my online life and space. So I revisited my accounts and changed a lot of settings. I also went into my generic DM folders (which I rarely check, to be honest) and deleted a bunch of unsolicited messages—the kind that are so obviously from bots. I deleted them all, most without really reading anything. If it looked like a bot, it was deleted.

Similarly, all the "Hello dear" messages were deleted instantly. If I don't know you, I'm not your "dear" in any way, shape, or form, and you definitely haven't earned the right to call me that. I went through each account and realized that I should have done this long ago, and it made me think of tagging. Weird, I know, but bear with me.

Years ago, my godbrother put an ad online for his NYC apartment. From what he told me, it went something like this:

*You have paint; I have a blank wall.*

I'm sure it was more involved than that, but that's what I remember most, because it was so simple. He basically wanted a graffiti artist to "tag" his blank kitchen wall, so he advertised for it. He found the right artist, and in a matter of hours had a one-of-a-kind piece of street art on his wall. Pretty cool, right? Well as he was explaining the story to us, he used the word "tagging," which was the first time I had heard of it. (I told you I wasn't hip.)

So as I deleted these random DMs from my social media accounts and thought about the troll who sent me an email, I realized that it was a form of "tagging" for them to be able to just write whatever they wanted on my "walls" online.

I wouldn't let someone come into my house and say whatever they wanted or write on my walls, so why would I allow it online? Suddenly, my empowerment grew in force, and I realized that my social media is there for me to engage with people who genuinely want to engage, civilly and respectfully, the way I would engage with them. It's also there for me to share my work and my life. So if a person feels it's their "right" to say whatever they want to me on my social media "walls," it's no different than them walking into my house, uninvited, and saying it to my face. I won't allow it in person, so I won't allow it online either. Delete.

Adopting a "no tagging allowed" mentality is powerful, and it's definitely part of the Fuck It! Lifestyle. Using the delete button instead of engaging keeps your response out of the reactive "fuck you!" territory. There's simply a swipe and tap of the finger: Delete.

To take it a step further, you can also use the "block" and "snooze" options, which are just as empowering and can be a lot of fun. (Seriously, try it out. You can thank me later.)

The bottom line is this: Your online life is its own radio station, and you get to control the dial. Don't like the song? Change it. Tired of the ads? Turn it off. You get to control what you let into your life and environment. Fuck It! and give it a go.

## Echoes offer nothing new

Of course, wielding this power can ruffle a few feathers, and that's okay. I think the only area that gives me pause or cause for concern is whether I'm creating an echo chamber online for myself. I don't want to do that because echoes offer nothing new. In fact, they often distort the original messaging over time.

Creating an echo chamber means that I'm silencing the voices that disagree with me simply because they disagree. I don't think that's right on multiple levels, but the two most important to me are:

1.  Disagreement is good for discussion and progress as long as it remains respectful and is based in fact.
2.  Echo chambers are boring.

Let's start with how boring they can be. Have you ever been at a party and looked around the room and saw everyone looking the same? I have. Years ago, I went to a Christmas party, and when I walked in, I instantly felt like I was back in college. All the women's outfits looked like they went shopping together at the same two stores while all the men were in some variation of the same "uniform." As a former fashion buyer, this was simply rather boring. I also suddenly felt a tiny bit worried about how the night would unfold. While it was a pleasant enough evening, I recall that every conversation with every person was 98% the same. The same questions, the same answers, and the same responses.

Echo chambers can be very boring.

Echo chambers also lead to a narrowing of belief. If you are only ever surrounded by people who think the same way you do, over time, that tunnel can only shrink because it has no opportunity for growth. Remember, there's nothing new and time will only serve to distort the original message.

More importantly, there's no opportunity for discussion or progress. I maintain that if you want two opposing sides to get together and find solutions for conflict, they *both* have to be at the table. Whether the conflict is as big as war or as small as siblings sharing a bedroom, if one side is left out, then the opportunity for connection is lost. In order to bridge any gap, commonalities have to be identified and then built on. Of course, I need to reiterate the importance of respect and truth, because without those two things, no connection or discussion is even possible to begin with.

Ultimately, echo chambers aren't good for growth. They're not good for connection. They're boring, and they're not something you should feel you need to engage in simply because everyone else around you is doing it.

Honestly, that can be the worst thing about echo chambers: choosing to live in an echo chamber because someone in our life is telling us to or shaming us into it—even indirectly. This may sound like, "I can't believe you watch that show," or "You're *still* listening to *that* podcast?" Those are often the hardest echo chambers to step out of. If you're there, I'm sorry. Know that you can change it.

In fact, this may be the perfect opportunity for you to embrace the Fuck It! Lifestyle and do what you need to do to stay connected, learning, and open to life and all it has to offer.

At the end of the day, your online community is your home, your home is your home, and your mind is your home. If any of those spaces have become something you don't like or don't want—or that feel out of alignment with you and your true self—you have the power to say "Fuck It!" and make them what you want.

If you only want to follow gardening, home, or travel accounts online, so be it! If you only want to follow comedians, have at it! There's no rule that says you must "follow back" if you don't want to. If you use social media for business, you've probably been told the same things I've been told, including the importance of following back. It's baloney. Half of the time, accounts that may be following you only start following you to get the follow back, and then they unfollow you. It's all a game. And Fuck It!—I'm 50 and tired of games. I follow who I want to follow, and I engage where I want to engage. Sometimes it creates incredible friendships. Other times it falls flat. Both are okay.

Ultimately, you don't have to justify your choices to anyone as long as you're not imposing on others (seriously, don't do that—it's really bad juju), taking advantage of others, lying, or being a jerk. Your life is yours. You don't have to explain to anyone why you only like following accounts about bread and cake.

For me, engagement online is the only reason to be online (that and a little escapism through the aforementioned gardening, home, and travel accounts). If I can't engage in at least a somewhat meaningful way, I don't need to do it. And if someone is making my online experience less than what I want it to be, then the delete, block, and snooze buttons are my superpower. Because... Fuck It!

## Chapter 4

# Getting Into the 'Pause

The 'Pause. The... men-o-pause. If you're 50, it's on the horizon if it's not already here yet. And it's a whole thing. As I write this, my 29–30-day, like-clockwork monthly cycle, which has been absent for the past two months, has decided to show up like a friend who's just back from an extended all-expenses-paid holiday in Tahiti and wants to tell me everything. *Sigh.*

I don't care how old you are, you're never ready for it. According to the experts, menopause begins sometime between ages 45 and 55, and is defined as twelve consecutive months without a period (just in case you didn't know). You can ask your mom, your sister, your grandmother, even your great-grandmother when they started menopause, and you can have a rough idea in your mind that it's coming, but until you actually have that first missed period, and then the second, you aren't ready for it.

Furthermore, as you enter this phase of your life and you miss a couple periods, you're definitely not ready for your period to randomly reappear (completely off schedule) and ruin your pajamas. After close to forty years of being able to plan for it, suddenly all planning goes out the window and you're left with question marks lingering in the air above your head.

How long will it last?

What about cramps?

When will it come back?

Will it come back?

Can I get rid of my "period underwear" now? (You know the ones I'm talking about, with the loose elastic and ripped seams. The ones you save for that time of the month, because why ruin a good pair?)

Also, now you're contemplating these questions:

What about hormones?

What about pregnancy protection? (I mean, surely you can't get pregnant now, right? Wrong. I have a friend who got pregnant pre-menopausal in her 50s. Yup, that's what I said. Fifties.)

So what do you do? More importantly, why don't we talk about it more? Why does it feel like it's relegated to some back corner of a dark room that only women who have gone before us can discuss in hushed tones with knowing looks on their faces?

In my mind, as I wrote that, I saw a bunch of women in their 60s and 70s sitting around a table and just laughing and laughing, sharing stories, drinking whatever they desire, and not giving a fuck. It's a rite of passage, this club. It's something you have to earn through decades of monthly bleeding, cramping, and bloating, until their cessation becomes the invisible ID card you carry to get through the door. (Which is unlike the very real and very unsolicited card AARP decides to send you when turning 50 lurks around the corner.)

Being on the outside of the door, however, it all feels a bit... well, taboo. We don't talk about what happens when our bodies and hormones change to such an extent that the thing that "made us a woman" is now absent from our lives.

*Wait, does this mean I'm not a woman anymore?*

Of course it doesn't, but I wouldn't be surprised if others had that thought or feeling based on what we're taught growing up. I know I did. Since "getting your period" means "you're a woman now"—what does losing your period mean? *Double sigh.*

## Plucking away

As if that's not bad enough, there's another surprise that can come with the 'Pause: more hair! To be specific, chin hair. At least for me. Somewhere in my 40s, I noticed a few stragglers popping up on my voluminous chin. It was easy enough to pluck them away. One or two a week, nothing major.

Now, on the cusp of diving full-on into the 'Pause, it seems that my hair follicles have banded together to create an insurrection on the bottom of my face. They've even adopted the wartime strategy of "divide and conquer"!

No longer relegated to the inch of space below my chin, I am finding rogue hairs along my jawline, up by my ears, and even a couple on my cheek. And they're not peach fuzz! Just as the 'Pause isn't readily discussed, nobody tells you about the army of coarse, darkly-colored (or white!) hairs that are going to lead a revolt on your face seemingly overnight. Winner winner, chicken dinner!

How did we go from soft, fuzzy hairs giving us a faint glow in a backlit picture to Hagrid's beard's cousin trying to relocate to a new home on our face? And don't get me started on all the ways we are told to remove said stragglers. You can:

Pluck.

Thread.

Wax.

Shave.

Zap.

Shock.

Burn.

Melt.

Bleach.

I'm sure there are more ways that I don't even know about, too. All of them take on the approach of a full assault on your face. Personally, I started waxing a few years ago, but Covid had me move on to plucking and tweezing. What used to last a week now barely lasts a couple days. How is it that my body suddenly has all the energy in the world to rapidly grow the randomest hair in the randomest of places but has no energy to stay up past 10:30 p.m.?

Welcome to 50.

And don't get me started on the rogue extra-long nose hair or eyebrow hair that shows up every once in a while as if it's a child peeking around the corner on Christmas morning. If you haven't had a rogue hair yet... just wait. It's on its way, and it will also arrive seemingly overnight. I've even had an eyelash go rogue and grow double in length!

Of course, constant plucking is a hassle, and I've since moved on to trying out a home IPL (Intense Pulsed Light) device that has gotten really good reviews. My hair might be a bit too blonde for it though. I don't know. I'm only on week three as I write this. I'd add that I never thought I would take a razor to my face the way I saw my dad do as I was growing up, but since that's what the IPL requires... here we are.

Again, welcome to 50!

I could say "fuck it" as many have done before me and just let it grow. But the Fuck It! Lifestyle is not about giving up and throwing in the towel, or not caring and letting everything go by the wayside. The Fuck It! Lifestyle is about getting clear on what matters to you and caring more. It means caring with intention and deliberate focus, prioritizing, and letting the rest fall away.

Personally, I care that when my double chin rubs against another part of my body, it doesn't feel like a cactus. Or random scraps of sandpaper. Or little needle tips. So Fuck It! I'm going to try and zap them away every week for the next six months. We'll see what happens. Thank you, hormones.

## To hormone or not to hormone

Now that you're on the verge of the 'Pause, what do you do about hormones?

As women, we're told we can go on replacement hormones to ease the transition. Replacement hormones come in a lot of different varieties and delivery methods, though, so what do you do? It all seems a bit overwhelming to navigate, to be honest.

I'm not a doctor, so I'm not going to tell you what to do. Heck, I don't even know what I'm going to do when that conversation comes.

What I *do* know is that every woman—every *body*—is different. I know women who have taken hormones and women who have not taken hormones. I know women who have had success in both camps and women who have not had success with anything. I know women who feel certain that they developed cancer as a result of their decision to take hormones and women who finally found health, life, and freedom again in making that same decision.

This is not a decision to take lightly, and it involves a lot of research, discussion, and time. What you choose to do is entirely up to you. Much like the rest of the focus of this book, the 'Pause is an opportunity for you to say "Fuck It!" and do what's best for you.

The short answer, therefore, is: When it comes to hormones, you do you, boo. (But... please talk to your doctor, too.)

## Pausing in a different way

I always thought it was weird that it's called meno*pause*. But now that I'm peeking behind that curtain, I decided to look it up. (Yes, I'm a word nerd.) "Menopause" is derived from the Greek words: menos and pausis, where menos means month, and pausis means to cease. So literally, it's the monthly ceasing. We just use the word "pause" a bit differently today, which I think could actually apply better here.

Over the past decade, I have somewhat lived in dread of menopause because it signaled the end of possibility for me. That possibility was the opportunity to have a biological child and build a family. It's only in the last couple of years that I have both accepted and embraced my reality, and even come to a healthy (possibly happy) understanding and acceptance. It still twinges a little bit sometimes though, if I'm honest. (Especially when I watch the *Mamma Mia!* movies.) And yet it's okay that it twinges, because it's the seeming finality of it all that was the culprit in my dread.

Let me explain.

As a woman, for most of my life I have subconsciously broken time down into three stages: pre-menstruation, menstruation, and post-menstruation. In fact, I think if we're honest, most of us do this, albeit less consciously. Through various means (advertising, media, etc.), as women, we are often taught that our worth is tied up in our achieving the pinnacle of what it means to be a woman: having kids. This then implies that the menstruation years are our era of greatest worth. This can also imply that once we hit menopause, our worth plummets.

Nothing could be further from the truth. Nothing.

In other cultures, mostly tribal, a woman's worth increases with age. Her life experience becomes increasingly more valuable, not less. She is more valued, more respected, and more important. In my opinion, the image of the "wise old woman" is vastly more exciting than the "tired old hag." More importantly, it's much nearer to the truth.

In order to get there, we have to shift our perspective and thinking around our worth—around women's worth—in our society. And then we have to act on it. Because there is nothing more magnetic, powerful, and engaging than a woman who knows who she is, stands in her boots, knows her worth, and lives from that place. The woman who can say "Fuck It!" to the world around her when it's feeding her bullshit about who she *should* be is the one that changes the world, even if it's only her world, which is more than enough.

So instead of thinking of it as a time of ceasing, as the Greek translation implies, I'm personally going to embrace the word "pause" the way I understand it colloquially and see it as a time in which my body is going to take a pause to adjust some things. It's going to pause as it figures out how it's going to function in a new way, and I'm going to flow with the pause (no pun intended) to allow it to do so. The 'Pause is not an ending, it's merely a shift. A shift that requires a pause. Meno-pause.

# Chapter 5

# Baseline: The Base That Matters

Speaking of shifting how we think about things, 50 comes with its own "to do" list of health-related items. Did you know?

In truth, I've been chipping away at this list since I turned 40. A year before my 40th birthday, I got divorced. My ex-husband was a doc, so I had been around the medical world for the better part of a decade while we were married. Additionally, when I was 34, my father had a massive stroke, so that also thrust the world of medicine into my life. As such, I learned a lot.

Over the years, I learned more about medicine, tests, and my own health than I ever would have otherwise. Thankfully, I am a generally healthy person. With the exception of an onslaught of random injuries over the past eight years, I've been conventionally healthy. I also get a yearly physical, know all my numbers, and focus on building relationships with my healthcare providers. As a result, I know my baseline, and more importantly, I know when something is wrong.

This is where 50 comes into play. If you don't know your baseline by 50, it's a good idea to prioritize it. *Collectively,* women are worse about attending to health issues than men. For example, statistically we know that women don't go to the hospital fast enough when having a heart attack. We also know that there are stereotypes around women and pain that have often led to medical professionals diminishing a woman's pain report. This means that even when women *do* show up, they can be dismissed. *Ugh.* I wish this weren't the case, but it is. However, since we know this is what's happening, we can do something to change it… and we should. (This is a good "should" by the way.)

This is where knowing your baseline comes in.

Knowing your baseline will allow you to speak differently to a healthcare professional and advocate for yourself in a way that will invite them to actually listen (more on the importance of advocacy in a minute). The more women that do this, the more chance we have of changing the stereotypes and statistics.

If, for example, you know your baseline blood pressure is typically on the low end, then when you go to the doctor or hospital with a concern, you can say, "Well, my 'normal' is X, so this is high for me." Or vice versa. Otherwise, without knowing your baseline, a healthcare professional could easily dismiss your concern as "normal" or suggest it is related to something else. Not good.

## Advocacy

Years ago, my doctor taught me something very important that has been critical for me when dealing with the medical world: *Know yourself and be your own best advocate.* In the same way you might advocate for your child—or your aging parents—you need to advocate for yourself. To do that effectively, you need to know your body. To know your body well, you need to know your medical baseline. Without knowing your baseline, it will be harder to advocate for yourself.

Unfortunately, women don't often advocate for themselves in general. Why? Well, the short answer is because we're not taught to. In fact, we're often subliminally taught not to. See if any of these phrases sound familiar to you:

*Don't rock the boat.*

*Don't rattle the cage.*

*Don't take up space.*

*Don't be loud.*

*Don't make a scene.*

*Don't cause trouble.*

*Don't be different.*

*Blah, blah, blah.*

If you didn't relate to one of those phrases, I am guessing you have a different one you could add to the list.

Historically, a woman speaking up was often derided. So why would we speak up for ourselves in the doctor's office if we don't feel we can speak up for ourselves anywhere else in life without being penalized? Understandably, you might think: *Well, certainly this isn't true with female doctors.* Well, not necessarily. Though it's gotten better in recent years, in my personal experience I've had more female healthcare professionals dismiss my self-advocacy than male healthcare professionals. That makes me sad to say, but it's true.

Knowing your baseline and being able to speak about it in a thoughtful way is one of the best things you can do for yourself. Even then, however, your self-advocacy can be dismissed. To me, I take that as a sign that I can't work with this professional, and I find someone else.

By knowing your baseline and practicing self-advocacy, you can also help change the system for all of us. In this way, we can say "Fuck It!" to all the stereotypes out there about women and healthcare. We can collectively grab those reins and take back the power to be in control of our own health and wellness. We can also better embrace aging by knowing more about our bodies and what they may need, so that they can better carry us forward in the decades to come. It's not about growing old—it's about growing old and being healthy along the way, which is a much better way to age.

## Grand slams are overrated

When it comes to our health after 50, wow, things can be different. Firstly, our hormones are the co-pilot of this ship, now. Accept it. I have a friend who is ten years ahead of me on this path, and the stories she has told me about being hot, then cold, then hot again, all within a matter of minutes leave me feeling overwhelmed. I already fear the night sweats because I have always hated sleeping hot.

When I spent a summer studying in Spain during my junior year in college, I think I got an average of three to four hours of sleep a night. I wish I could say it was because I was out having fun and being young. Alas, it wasn't. It was because Madrid in July averaged 100°–120°F! I imagine those nights were a bit like a woman going through menopause sitting up at night staring at the wall because she was too hot to lie down and have a higher percentage of her skin's surface area touching something. So while my friend is on the other side of it, I have that to look forward to. Yay.

Other older female friends have reported more adventures that their hormones have navigated for them, including: weight gain, exhaustion, headaches, skin issues, mood swings and irritability, dryness (yes, *that* dryness), and genuine malaise. There should be a road sign for entering this stage of life:

### Fun Times Ahead!
### (Just kidding—buckle up, buttercup!)

However, even though this may be on the horizon as you turn 50, it's not a foregone conclusion that you will experience any of these symptoms. Furthermore, as I said in the last chapter, if you can shift your thinking to see menopause as a temporary pause and not a life sentence, you will be much better for it.

So where does knowing your baseline matter in all of this? Well, it's about realizing it's more important to "round the bases" than to aim for a grand slam. Firstly, grand slams are way too much pressure, and who wants to deal with that after 50? Secondly, and more importantly, grand slams are really rare. Aiming for a grand slam and repeatedly not achieving it will keep you from enjoying rounding the bases.

Yes, you can enjoy aging when it comes to your health. Here's why I enjoy it: I find it exciting to see if I can move the needle. Focusing on specific aspects of my health and getting confirmation that something has changed for the better is incredibly rewarding and motivating.

For most of our lives, many of us have spent a lot of our time focused on changing something about ourselves because a lot of marketing is based on telling you that you suck as you are. Did you realize that? The messaging roughly boils down to: *Buy this product so that you can no longer suck.*

But now at 50, you can say "Fuck It!" and choose your own adventure. (Who remembers those books?) Knowing your baseline lets you choose where you want to focus your attention, one base at a time.

- **First base:** Want more sleep? Or better sleep? Set up a system that allows you to do just that—from changing your bedtime to assigning nighttime chores to other people in your life, or anything else you can think of to protect your sleep time.
- **Second base:** Want to walk outside with a friend instead of going to the gym? Strap on those hiking boots or walking shoes, call a friend, and get walking! (And don't forget to suspend your gym subscription, if you have one.)
- **Third base:** Want to drink less alcohol but are worried what your social group will think? Fuck It! (And maybe fuck them, if they'd judge you for this.) Experiment at home with some

fun, non-alcoholic beverages and bring your own to the next party. Sip it and smile, knowing that you won't be hungover tomorrow.

The bottom line is: *You* get to decide what you want to focus on when it comes to your health, ideally through knowing your baseline and with the help of your doctor.

Now, if you turn 50 and suddenly think, "Oh crap! Now I have to get healthy," you're missing the point. It's not a one-and-done day, year, or decade. 50 is a milestone moment in time that you can take advantage of to gather good data and make some changes, if you want to.

If you don't want to, that's fine too. I still suggest getting your baseline done, though, because it's just good to have. Plus, it can only help you properly advocate for yourself as you grow older. Think of it as a "Fuck It! Tool" in your toolbox. The more data you have, the more easily you can decide where to say Fuck It! and change something, as well as where you can simply move on.

Of course, there are two things that most healthcare professionals suggest as mandatory once you hit 50 (or sometimes 40 or 45): Mammograms and Colonoscopies. (I capitalized them to add a bit of gravitas.) In America, the CDC suggests biannual mammograms for women aged 50+, but other healthcare organizations say 40 is better. For colonoscopies, the CDC recommends you start screening at 45. This could change, of course, but the bottom line is: If you're 50, you should have both done if you haven't already.

## The best sleep you'll ever have

Let's start with the colonoscopy. It's the best sleep you'll ever have. Seriously. I still think back on it and wish I could sleep like that again. In fact, I think that if everybody got a deep, medicine-induced sleep like that once a month, we'd live in a much happier world. Before they put me under, the anesthesiologist said those words to me: This'll be the best sleep you've ever had. I scoffed. I mean, I had some pretty amazing sleeps in my life when I was younger. When I woke up, however, I realized he wasn't lying. Suddenly, all the prep and fear of the experience made me recategorize the sleep as a "reward" for having gone through it. It was a heady and relaxed moment, until it wasn't.

"You need to pass gas, Martina."

I replied groggily, "What?! Here? Now?"

Of course, the story in my head went more like: *If you think I'm farting here, in the open, with only thin curtains separating me from the people around me, you're wrong. That's disgusting!*

Then suddenly, "Pppffffffffftttttt," my butt chimed in with its own airy opinion. This was followed by sounds I've never heard before. It was as if the brass section of an orchestra was warming up in turns. First the trombone, then the trumpet. Oh, and wait, here comes the tuba!

"Good. Keep going," the nurse said nonchalantly, as she exited through the curtain, leaving the expected gap so everyone can see in.

My face was crimson, but I'm not going to lie, it felt so good to fart. In a colonoscopy, they fill your system with air so that they can actually see inside. They literally inflate you like a balloon. So yes, you will (and have to) pass gas when it's over. They don't let you go home if you don't.

It doesn't change how embarrassing it is, though. I wish someone had told me more about what actually happens so that I could be prepared. Hence, I'm sharing it with you here. You're welcome. (And Fuck it! Go ahead and fart! You need to.)

Of course, most people also know that the prep for a colonoscopy is... let's use the word: grueling. If you are a stranger to your toilet, you won't be for long. For me, though, the harder part was getting all of the liquid into my system to allow it to do its magic. It's sickeningly sweet, and the consistency was like drinking oil. Each sip made me gag. I remember pinching my nose to try and get more of it down, a trick from childhood when you had to eat or drink something that you didn't like. It didn't help.

No amount of information prepared me for the process that is a colonoscopy. Thankfully, I'm currently on a 7–10 year cycle, which means I don't have to endure it again until I'm 55–57. I'm quite sure, however, that I will be daydreaming about that sleep until then.

## Squish, squish, squish

When I turned 40, I had a scare with my mammogram. There was a spot. The office called me back to schedule an ultrasound so that they could further investigate before possibly scheduling a biopsy. It was three days before I could get in for an appointment, and they were some of the longest three days of my life.

All sorts of questions loomed in my brain. Questions for which there were no answers. Or at least for which I had no answers. When I went in for the ultrasound, I was greeted by a doctor instead of a nurse. He would be conducting the ultrasound himself as the nurse assisted. To me, this signaled a seriousness that only served to increase my worry and fear. In hindsight, I understood that it was meant to decrease my worry, as it removed the delay between the scan and the scan results. The doctor was able to tell me in the moment what his findings were. Thankfully, he wasn't concerned, and the possible biopsy was canceled.

Mammograms are part of life as a woman, thankfully. Even though most women I've spoken to experience at least a little fear while waiting for their results, they all complain about the exam itself. I don't blame them. I mean, if men had to place their penis on a clear acrylic slab while another slab of the same size pressed down on it until it was squished like a pancake, I feel certain they'd invent something else.

But we endure it because it's helpful. Mammograms often catch things before they become a problem. We raise our arms above our heads, allow someone with cold, gloved hands to lift our breast onto an acrylic plate, and maneuver it into a position for maximum squish. Then we watch as the other acrylic plate moves closer and closer to our skin before it comes into contact and is tightened enough to create the widest possible squished boob. We breathe in and hold our breath so that the image is as perfect as it can be. And then we repeat it again, and again, and again, before moving to the other breast.

It's all over in a matter of minutes, of course, and it's a life-saving test—one that is an integral piece of our baseline as we grow older. But it doesn't change the fact that all the squishing, exposure, and contortion going on is a little humbling.

On my last mammogram, the nurse turned to me and said, "Well, here we go!" as if we were off to the races or something as she reached for my right breast and moved it into its first position. In my peripheral vision, I watched my boob being squished until she told me to hold my breath so she could take the pic. I remember thinking to myself how grateful I am that this technology exists, and also how absolutely ridiculous it is that I'm standing with one arm still in a robe while the rest of me is completely exposed.

As I contorted my torso into all the different positions to create the maximum squishy view of my breast tissue, I said to her, "This robe really isn't doing much..." To which she replied, "I know honey, but we try."

It then dawned on me that the robe was a tiny vestige of dignity for what was mostly an incredibly vulnerable experience, both emotionally and physically. I'm glad they try. I'm glad I can still contort my body to get the best view of the tissue, and I'm glad someone invented the boob squisher.

## What is health anyway?

Health is not a "one size fits all" endeavor—it never was. The problem is that we've had countless people tell us it is in order to sell their wares. The only thing that might possibly fit the "everyone" bill is a slight variation of something 90s personality Susan Powter said.

If you're reading this book around the time that it was written, you are probably close to 50 and familiar with Susan Powter. If you don't know who I'm talking about, look her up. Susan rose to fame in the 1990s with her infomercials. She was a nutritionist and personal trainer from Australia who is famous for her short, platinum hair and the tagline, *Stop the Insanity!,* which referred to her actionable message about health: *Eat, Breathe, Move.*

Susan hit on a trifecta for health that was simple and could be applied to everyone. We all have to eat, we all have to breathe, and we all have to move. This is true for every human on the planet, in one way or another. It's actually true for more than humans, but this isn't that book.

While Susan's message was both simple and direct, I would modify it as follows:

**You have to eat, you have to *sleep*, and you have to move.**

I've changed "breathe" to "sleep" because sleeping is an aspect of health around which you can actively make decisions, just as eating and moving are. Breathing (unless you are medically unable to in some way) is automatic. Yes, breathing can be an aspect of mindfulness, yoga, or other wellness modalities—in fact, it often is, for good reason. And yes, you could breathe more deeply or consciously, but for the most part, if you're alive, you're breathing. You don't have to think about it. You just do it... even if you could do it better.

Eating, moving, and sleeping, however, are habits that you can focus on and modify throughout the course of your life, and probably have. If there is a one-size-fits-all approach to good health, it includes eating, sleeping, and moving. These high-level categories are true for everyone. For good health, you have to eat (and drink water), you have to sleep, and you have to move. How you choose to do those things is up to you, and there is no lack of information out there to take advantage of this simple truth. This is why the "wellness" industry is a multi-billion dollar enterprise.

There seem to be new diets, new programs, new workouts, and new supplements (to name a few) cropping up every day. They all promise to be "the one" solution for you. However, they all make promises that they may not be able to keep, because there is actually no "one" solution for everybody. There is only the solution for you. Trust me, I've wasted many hundreds—if not thousands—of dollars on different programs, powders, and pills over several decades. At the end of the day, there is one simple truth about being, getting, or staying healthy:

**You have to eat.**
**You have to sleep.**
**You have to move.**

Only *you* can decide what that looks like for you. Only *you* can know what will work and what won't work for you. Only you get to decide what "eat, sleep, move" means for you. If it's Crossfit, have at it. If it's not Crossfit, don't do it. If it's swimming, or walking, or tennis, or dance, it's up to you how you want to move. Your good health is dependent on your decisions, and your success is probably dependent on trial and error. What I know for sure is that if you enjoy it, you're more likely to stick with it.

Only you will know what works. Nobody else can tell you (or promise you) that their "solution" is *the* solution for you just because it was the solution for them. It's up to you to find what works for you and to be open to new ideas and/or changes over time (if you want to be).

When I have clients who say they want to get healthier, they often express it with resignation. They rarely seem happy or excited about it.

When I ask them why they are making health a goal, their answer is often, "Because I *should*..." So I change the question, and the conversation usually looks like this:

*Client: I need to start working out.*

*Me: Why?*

*Client: Because I'm supposed to.*

*Me: Why?*

*Client: Why? What do you mean, "Why?"*

*Me: Well, it doesn't sound like you want to work out, so... why are you saying that you're supposed to?*

*Client: Because I'm not getting any younger.*

*Me: None of us are.*

*Client: And because I just... I should.*

*Me: Again, why?*

*Client: To be healthier.*

*Me: Ah, that's different from "I need to start working out," though, isn't it? What if you said, "I need to get healthier?" Or even better: "I want to be healthier?"*

*Client: That sounds better.*

*Me: Or... feel healthier?*

*Client: That's more accurate.*

*Me: Try it on for size.*

*Client: I want to feel healthier.*

*Me: Bingo! Now, what will help you feel healthier?*

*Client: I don't know.*

*Me: Okay. Let's explore that and figure out what works for you.*

It's usually at this point that I can see a difference in their face or hear a difference in their voice. It's no longer something to dread because it's now something to engage with. "Healthier" may include working out, but it doesn't have to. It could include taking walks in the forest or dancing with your girlfriends on a Friday night. Healthier may include some form of movement, because we've identified that as one of the three aspects of good health. However, "healthier" can mean whatever they want or need it to mean, and more often than not it typically means *I want to feel more vibrant, more alive... more free!*

Now that's a sentiment I can get behind, and it's an inherent part of Fuck It!

Standing in your boots is an invitation to truly live. On your path to more vibrancy, if something causes you dread or makes you feel resigned, you are less likely to do it, sustain it, or engage with it. It really is that simple.

So if good health is about feeling more vibrant, find what you love, and do that. If you don't know how you love to move, I have a trick for you: Think about how you liked to move when you were a kid. Did you love riding your bike? Dancing? Playing soccer? Chances are if you loved it then, you'll love it now—or something similar. Plus, the upside of the multi-billion dollar industry is that there is probably a class or a group for the thing you love. You just have to do a little digging to find it.

Being healthy—feeling vibrant—involves how you choose to eat, sleep, and move. So focus on the foods you love that are healthier, the amount of sleep as well as the sleep environment you actually need, and how you enjoy moving best (and yes, sex can be quite the workout, if you want it to be), and say Fuck It! to the rest. These three things are the clearest paths toward better health, especially when you combine them with knowing and understanding your baseline.

Frankly, even though some of the things we have to do as we age can feel overwhelming, I think we're lucky. We're lucky to have the technology to discover anomalies and catch them early, especially if it means a longer and healthier life.

Using the tools available to us to learn more about our bodies is a gift, not a burden. Understanding your baseline is the best way to advocate for yourself, for your health, and for your future. If not now, when?

My invitation to you is simple: Say Fuck It! even if it feels scary, and do it anyway. Your 60- or 70-year-old self will be glad you did. Here's to your good health!

# Chapter 6

# Vitamin Z

Ahhh... sleep. As we've just discussed, sleep is one of the three important aspects of health. We need good sleep and enough of it to be healthy.

But, you're 50 now, so welcome to the love/hate relationship between sleep, aches and pains, and your bladder! Actually, I think the bladder issue started around 47, but may also be the result of prioritizing my hydration. Similarly, the aches and pains could be caused by the random injuries and surgeries I've had in the past eight years, but it all counts. Why? Because I have friends who have reported similar symptoms without the excuses of hydration and injury. Now, like menopause, you may not experience any of these things. Maybe your bladder won't start waking you up until you're 60! If that's the case, lucky you!

Frankly, I think turning 50 is when we get to unapologetically announce: "I'm going to bed" even if it's 7:30 p.m. and the dishes are still in the sink. And "bed" doesn't have to mean sleep. It can simply mean: *I'm done with today and would like it to end peacefully with things I love, like a magazine, a bath, trashy TV, or, in fact, sleep.* Of course, if you have dependents (kids, pets, aging parents), it's kind of a pipe dream. But I like to dream.

Though it currently seems to be changing, throughout most of my life western society's messaging around sleep has not had our best interests in mind. I may even go so far as to say it's been harmful, toxic, and deceptive. By the time we're 50, our "Culture of Do" has encouraged us to minimize sleep over the past three or four decades of our lives. In college, it seemed to make sense. Maybe in our 20s it also made sense on the weekends, but once we hit 30, it no longer made sense. And then some of us started having kids, and sleep became... "What's sleep?" Of course, this phrase is also attributable to: marriage/relationships, work, stress, finances, and many other things. So basically: adulting.

Coffee or caffeine quickly became the co-pilot of our lives somewhere in our 20s when we learned to translate a sleep deficit into a badge of honor.

"How much sleep did you get last night?"

"Oh, me? Let me think—it must have been only four or five hours!"

"Wow, lucky you!"

"I know, right?"

*Yawn.*

*Yawn.*

The truth is, numerous studies show undeniably that sleep deprivation is terrible for our health. Chronic lack of sleep contributes to an increased risk of: hypertension, diabetes, obesity, depression, heart attack, and stroke. I'm not kidding—look it up. That's quite a list, especially when you add the loss of the estrogen that has been protecting our hearts up until now. To quote a famous Charlie: Good Grief!

It's true. In our 30s, we may have slept less for lots of reasons, many of which were within our control (if we stopped long enough to think about it). But now at 50, we're sleeping less because of things that are more outside of our control. And it only has the potential to worsen as we get older. Yikes!

## Don't let the sun go down on me...

When I was 26, I had a knee surgery that went terribly wrong. I ended up in the hospital for a week on IV blood thinners with round-the-clock monitoring so that I didn't die. Thankfully, the hospital had the sense to put me in my own room. Why? Because the floor I was on (not the ICU, but more critical than basic) had a population of patients whose average age was probably somewhere between 75 and 80. They all needed more eyes on them for whatever brought them to the hospital, just as I needed more eyes on me.

The kicker is, among the elderly, there's a phenomenon called "sundowning"—which means that when the sun goes down, the patients wake up! Sundowning is a symptom that predominantly affects people with Alzheimer's and dementia. However, it is a term that has also been used colloquially to explain the phenomena of waking up as the sun goes down.

For the last two years of his life, my father was in a care home as his level of care exceeded that which we could safely provide in our house. He didn't have any sleep issues, but I did ask one of the nurses about sundowning and whether it was a thing beyond Alzheimer's and dementia. (See? It stuck with me for over 20 years.) She said yes. She explained to me that our internal clocks can become dysregulated, especially when we spend entire days indoors, which is one of the reasons why they try to keep a schedule for their patients. If a patient sleeps too much during the day, they can often have more difficulty sleeping at night and exhibit signs of sundowning.

Growing up, I also remember hearing my grandmother talk about her sleep habits. She said that the older she got, the less she slept, especially at night. As a kid, I remember thinking, *That will never happen to me—I love my sleep!* But now I see how it possibly could... if I don't take the steps to change it. Though sleep habits typically change as we age, it's not a foregone conclusion that they have to get worse. (Hooray!)

Now that we're 50, the key is to figure out how to manage your relationship with sleep so that you don't fall into this stereotype of aging. It's the perfect time to say Fuck It! and figure out how to make your sleep a priority, whether that means changes to your bedtime routine, your sleep environment, or when and how you wake up. (This is especially important if the people around you might not necessarily be on the same page. Just a heads up!)

## Wet noses and bookends

One of the magical things about having a dog or two is that they can be a natural alarm clock for you, if they're so inclined. Of course, there are some dogs that prefer the warmth and coziness of their bed (or yours!) to getting up and having to go outside to do their business. Especially on a cold morning. But that's not the situation in my home.

For the past 12 years, I have rarely had to set an alarm clock in the morning. Somewhere between 6 and 7:30 a.m. I will have two 50 lb dogs jump on my bed and stick their noses in my face or paw me. It's a lovely way to wake up.

I actually mean that.

For the mornings that I have an early client, I actually set a "just in case" alarm. On the rare occasion that the alarm wakes me up before the dogs, it's incredibly jarring. I'll take wet noses over obnoxious sounds any day. But I've always wondered, why do we set an alarm to wake up but do nothing to go to sleep?

A few years ago, when I decided to prioritize my sleep, I started setting a "bedtime" on my phone. After a certain hour, I became unreachable. I've long maintained that my devices are for my convenience, but I never actually used them to proactively create better habits around my sleep or anything else. As soon as I put the "bedtime" setting on my phone, I started to notice a difference. The lack of texts or calls coming through actually gave me some mental space. (Boundaries are magical creatures.) Once I had created that space, I made more changes to my sleep routine that I knew would serve me in the long run.

For starters, I decided to condition my body to sleep. This means that when I finally went to bed, I had three things I could choose to do: read a book or magazine, play sudoku, or listen to a yoga nidra guided meditation. (Have you tried yoga nidra? It's magical!) Additionally, I have three different "sleep" playlists that I cycle between. This simple act of focusing on environmental stimuli and behavioral habits in the moments before sleep has actually resulted in my body now recognizing the signals that it's time to sleep. It's great! (Unless, of course, one of the pieces of music is played elsewhere, as I recently experienced. I wondered why I was getting so relaxed and sleepy in the middle of the day! Oops.)

Now that my bedtime was "bookended" at both the start and at the finish, I could focus on the actual routine in between. I have to say that I haven't figured it all out yet. Some of my routine clashes with other things I have prioritized, like the aforementioned hydration. Plus, as a small business owner, sometimes I do have to skip it all and get back to my desk for something time sensitive late at night. But those are the exceptions, not the rule.

Building a routine you can sustain is key to getting your Vitamin Z. By doing this myself, I have moved the needle on my sleep from an average of under seven hours/night, to an average of almost eight hours/night... and on good nights, I can get closer to nine! I use devices to track it so that I have the data and can see that my baseline has shifted for the better! (A-hem, hint hint.)

## My sleeping fund

One of the biggest stressors when it comes to sleep is... money. Yup, we *all* worry about money on some level. Even people who seem to have a lot of money worry about money. Seems crazy, right? But it actually makes sense. Why? Because we live in a society whose messaging is all based on lack. The messages we receive daily in our media, advertising, and yes, even in religious houses, is that you *should* have more. Which translates to: *You don't have enough.*

It's messy, this "never enough" stuff. It puts everyone on the same playing field chasing more. This is why we have a Culture of Do.

Do more to get more.

Do more to be more.

Do more to be accepted, approved, loved... the list goes on and on. As a result, we stay awake at night chasing more, including more money. Because if we had more money, we could do and be all the things we're told we *should* be and do. Do you see the cycle? Do-be-do-be-do. (Could be a song, albeit a really depressing one.)

How do we say "Fuck It!" to this worrisome impact on our sleep, though? We're 50 now, surely we can get a better handle on this Do game. Surely we've earned our rest at night. Surely.

A few weeks ago, I saw someone (a celebrity, maybe? I don't remember) talk about their "Fuck You Fund." This is a bank account they set up so they would have the ability to say "fuck you" easily enough to anything that they didn't want to do. It was a fund for the freedom to say no. Pretty cool, right?

Well, when I was in my late 20s, after having gone through some serious issues in my marriage, I made what I called a "sleeping fund." This was something I needed in order to sleep at night. Mind you, it wasn't huge. At the time, I was working three jobs (one full-time and two part-time), as my then-husband couldn't work one. So money was tight, and at times not enough. But I would still put $1.00 a month in the fund, if I could.

In better months, I'd put in $50.

Some months I put in whatever change I could find. I remember one month I found a quarter on the ground in the parking lot where I worked, and I was so happy because I knew it was going right into my sleeping fund.

Did I sleep better at night? You bet I did!

Did I tell him about it? You bet I didn't!

I told my mom about it, though, and she would occasionally send me a $10 bill for my sleeping fund. When I got divorced, I pulled out my sleeping fund and used it to pay some bills. It went back to zero as I took out a loan and went to grad school.

When I graduated, I started it up again. And every month without fail, I put something in it. It's not huge, and it's certainly not the "three months of living expenses" that financial planners advise we have available just in case. But it's mine, and just knowing it's there helps me sleep better.

Interestingly, one of the things I have learned in mostly working with women for the past 15 years is that stress and fear can be significantly exacerbated from not having money set aside somewhere.

When I was at a friend's kid's birthday party many years ago, one of the moms there asked me what I did for a living. I was standing in a circle of five or six women, and I said, "I help people as a life coach. Most of my client base is made up of women in their 30s, 40s, or 50s." They all just stared at me, so I continued. "They come to me because they woke up one morning, looked around them and said, 'What the fuck! How did I get here? Who am I?' and then they tell a friend, and the friend refers them to me," I paused for effect, "And I help them reclaim who they are."

They all remained silent, most looking slightly down at the ground, and they all nodded. There was a knowing in that circle of women, a recognition that they could all relate to what I just said. And there was something else. Fear. Fear that it was true and fear that they could do nothing about it. Perhaps because of money, or maybe because of something else. Either way, there was fear that it was truer than they wanted to admit—or truer than they had realized, perhaps.

Fear is one of the greatest determinants of how well and how long we sleep. The bottom line is: If you're worried about money or anything else, for any reason, you're probably not sleeping well. And if you're not sleeping well—or sleeping enough—you're increasing your risk of some pretty serious health conditions and diseases.

If I could give any of those women, who were probably in their early 40s at the time, one piece of advice from everything I've learned over the years, it would be to say "Fuck It!" and protect your sleep. And make a sleeping fund.

## Chapter 7

# You Expect Me to Do What?!

If there's ever a moment to embrace "50 and Fuck It!" it's when it comes to expectations. Seriously. This is something that gets to all of us somewhere along the way, and it's also the most obvious use of the Fuck It! Tool. I mean, ever since we were younger, we've constantly been told what to do, what to wear, how to think, what to eat, and so on—who hasn't wanted to just say "fuck it!"? I can distinctly remember a time in my teens when I thought it would be easier to say "fuck it" than to do my homework. I was tired, it was late, and I simply had no more in me to give. A part of me thought I could do it in the morning. I was wrong. A tired teen at night is one thing. A tired teen in the morning is a zombie!

So I went to school, homework undone, and I hoped I could talk my way out of it. Even then, however, the Fuck It! was strong in me. I used it like the Force and allowed it to flow through me like a Jedi. I was tired, I didn't care, and that was that. Of course, I lost marks for it at the time. But in the grand scheme of things, I turned out alright. So Fuck It!

It wasn't the true Fuck It! though. It was a "fuck it" of not caring, not a Fuck It! of caring more intentionally and deliberately. It had a hint of the Fuck It! Manifesto about it, in that I prioritized my well-being and slept instead of staying up to do homework, but that's where the similarity ended.

Looking back, I don't know how I managed to get through my last two high school years with everything I did. I recently shared my junior/senior high school schedule with a friend who has a 12-year-old son, and she was somewhat shocked:

6:00 a.m.—Wake up, bathe, dress, eat

6:45/7:00 a.m.—Leave for school (6:45 if I was taking the bus, 7:10 if I was driving)

7:50–8:00 a.m.—Arrive at school

8:10 a.m.—Homeroom

8:20 a.m.—Classes began

11:15 a.m.—15-minute break, depending on your class schedule

11:30 a.m.—Class

12:30 p.m.—Lunch

1:15 p.m.—Classes

4:30 p.m.—Prep for sports

5:00 p.m.—Sports

6:15 p.m.—Eat something/anything (sometimes just a giant dill pickle!)

7:00 p.m.—Extracurricular activities, like play rehearsals

9:00 p.m.—Drive home

10:00 p.m.—Start homework

12:00/1:00 a.m—Go to bed

Of course, I didn't *have* to do sports or plays, but 1) I really loved them, and 2) if I didn't, how could I expect to get into college? Or at least a college of my choice? The pressure we put on kids is insane. Whenever I work with a high schooler on their college essay, I see it firsthand. They are absolutely shattered, trying to be everything they think they are *supposed to be*. The expectations they place on themselves as a result are beyond overwhelming. So though my teenage "fuck it" moment was not necessarily the same as the empowered, stand-in-your-boots Fuck It! I can look back on teenage me and smile. Hey, at least I got some sleep! Of course, my teachers didn't see eye-to-eye with me on this, as the expectation was that I'd do my homework. And I didn't. For which I expected to receive a bad grade. And I did. Life is easier when expectations are clearly spelled out. Most problems are a result of poorly communicated or identified expectations, of ourselves and others.

## Flexibility isn't just for yoga

Being flexible in what you expect of yourself is a superpower I bet you didn't know you had. If you knew someone was doing the best they could, would you be more willing to be flexible with them? I bet you would. So why not extend the same courtesy to yourself?

The problem is that we often treat others better than we treat ourselves, and it takes a fair amount of living to wake up and decide that's not how you want to be treated. Especially by your own hand. So how can we get more flexible in the expectations we have of ourselves?

I have a trick for this. But let's back up a little bit.

If you ask any of my closest friends, they will tell you that for much of my life, I have been pretty hard on myself. I used to say that I didn't play competitive sports because I don't like competing. But that's not 100% true. I didn't like competing with others, but I thrived on competing with myself. So team sports were not ideal for me, whereas solo sports definitely were. I was a massive tennis player when I was younger, and I was pretty good at it. Not great, mind you, but pretty good. Good enough to make the varsity team in high school as the number three or number four singles player (it went back and forth) and the number one doubles player with my partner.

I loved tennis because the person I was really trying to beat was myself. I wanted to be better than I was the day before. I wanted to learn how to "place" the ball on the other side of the net. I wanted to understand how I could change my grip and change a shot. Tennis was perfect for me. Yes, I wanted to win matches, but mostly I wanted to constantly get better, little by little.

As a result, I put some crazy expectations on myself and spoke to myself in a way that was anything but kind. I'd wager that most of my friends didn't know that at the time, but as I got older, my inner circle definitely started to see the kind of unreal expectations I held for myself and the crap I endured as a result. My marriage comes to mind, as most of my closest friends couldn't understand why I stayed for so long when it clearly wasn't getting better. But I had an expectation that I had made a vow, and I was going to see it through, no matter the consequences.

If it had been one of my friends, however, I would have wanted to see them make a different decision. I would have had better, more flexible expectations of my friend than I did of myself. It was only when it became a matter of survival that leaving my marriage became the only option. But I will share all of that in another book. What matters here is that my inflexible and unrealistic expectations of myself kept me in a very unhealthy situation for far longer than I should have stayed. (Yes, I said "should"—in this instance, it's appropriate.)

Fast forward to six years after my divorce, about a year after my first book came out. I had a conversation with one of my oldest friends in which she said something like this in response to my diminishing my accomplishment:

"Dude! Let's stop for a second. You need to realize that you *wrote a book*. You wrote a book! Not only that, but you wrote it, published it, sold it, and got press for it. A book! Do you know how few people in the world can say that? And how many want to, but can't? Stop being so hard on yourself."

While I don't remember what I said that led up to that moment, I do remember her words. They have stayed with me ever since. Sometimes, when we do something that seems to come naturally, we can diminish its value, to others and to ourselves. We have an expectation that since we did it, it's no big deal. But it is a big deal.

I wrote a book!

Not only that, but I published it, marketed it, sold it, and had articles written about it. I thought it wasn't a big deal. I thought it was "normal" for anyone to do, but it wasn't. When I spoke to another friend who had been in the marketing department of one of the "big five" publishing houses for almost 20 years and told her that in my first year (with my first book) I had "*only* sold about 1,000 copies," she was shocked. She said, "Do you know how hard that is to do?"

I didn't.

I diminished my success for two reasons: 1) I didn't know the statistics because I didn't research them, and 2) my expectations of myself were much higher than anything I would have asked of anyone else.

They were unrealistic, harsh, and actually unkind. I would never treat somebody the way I treated myself. And the kicker is, you'd think I would have learned all this after my divorce. But no, I'm human, and that means that sometimes I have to repeat things in order to get them. Once I got it, however, I created a trick that helps me remember the importance of flexibility in life, especially when it comes to expectations of myself and others. (I told you I had a trick for you.)

What's the trick?

Create a filter.

A filter is a question, or sometimes a statement, that allows you to pause and redirect. It creates flexibility and helps make your thoughts and actions more nimble. Then, if you want to create a filter on steroids, you add the Fuck It!

The more you use it and practice it, the easier it becomes.

The simplest version of a filter is often, "Would I say this to my best friend?" But I like to make it more engaging, so I changed it to: "Would I say this to my dog?"

Why my dog? Because he is 100% dependent on me, and it's one of the most unconditionally loving experiences I've ever been lucky enough to have in my life. For some of you, you're probably nodding your heads right now and thinking about your own dog(s), your kid(s), your cat(s), or any other living being in your life that fills the same role.

Additionally, it's possible that we *might* be willing to say something harsh or judgmental to our best friend, which is why I changed it. The dog scenario is so much cleaner. I have expectations of him, of course. Things like: don't pee in the house and don't chew up my shoes. These are basic expectations that he abides by because I took the time to teach him. My expectations were taught to him through clear communication, and he was given the flexibility of time to learn. What a compassionate way to live!

But we're not talking about basic expectations when we are looking at being unrealistic or harsh, especially with ourselves. We're talking about the unspoken, often insidious expectations we place on ourselves. Though many may have root causes, such as families of origin or societal systems, we're here to address our own patterns of behavior so we can free ourselves of the invisible shackles that keep us from living our best lives as who we are. Rigid expectations can be those shackles.

The key to unlocking them is the filter question.

By adding a filter question, you can create more flexibility around how you speak to yourself, and subsequently what you expect of yourself. Flexibility in yoga is great, but flexibility in expectations is fucking magical!

Then when you add the Fuck It! to that filter of flexibility, you're talking about a real superpower. Suddenly, decisions become easier and clearer because you care more with greater intention and focus on the things that really matter to you, and you care less about the fluff. It really doesn't get better than that. And here's the next magical thing: It translates to your relationships!

## Your expectations are not my emergency

We've probably all seen this meme/quote at some point, right: *Your lack of planning is not my emergency.* Now, what happens when we change "lack of planning" to "expectations"?

**Your expectations are not my emergency.**

Boom! Someone else's expectations do not constitute an emergency for you. In general, expectations need to be negotiated if they are going to be effective. Other than a job description (and sometimes even then), all expectations between two people, or two groups, or a group and a person, need to be negotiated, otherwise there will probably be disappointment.

Negotiation requires clear communication and a willingness to be flexible. In all my years of helping people, I can tell you that the biggest and most common issues I have seen all revolved around communication and expectations. Whether the expectations weren't stated, weren't agreed to, or simply weren't realistic, it didn't matter. What everyone focuses on when there is a divide is that the outcome wasn't what was desired or expected. We're all programmed to focus on the result without really looking at the events that led up to the result or the communication (or lack thereof) inherent in the events leading up to the result. However, if we focus on the communication—specifically communicating about and negotiating expectations—everything changes, and for the better.

## You can't say that!

Now that you're 50, my guess is you might be much more willing to call people out than you were just ten years ago, or even five. It's one of the most liberating things I've experienced as I've aged. And I know I'm not alone. So many of my friends along the way have shared some version of a meme on social media that goes like this: *I can't wait until I'm old and gray... so I can say anything I want!*

We all want the freedom to express ourselves and to call out rudeness in others, but as women, we typically feel that we shouldn't. We shouldn't, that is, until we are older (or old?) because then we can do it freely, and who's going to tell us not to? Our white hair says we've earned it. Plus, if they are upset, the meme implies that we don't care. Fuck it, right?

But that's not the Fuck It! we want to be using. We want to do something because we care more, not less. We want to use our Fuck It! for the moments that matter, that we've identified as being aligned with who we are.

How often have you wanted to say to someone, "No, I'm not going to do that," but didn't? How about listening to a committee chair assigning roles and responsibilities without first asking people what they want to do? I've been in those meetings, and I definitely wanted to raise my hand and say, "Fuck it, no, that's not what I signed up for," and just leave.

## Ask, don't task

Of course, being able to delegate is an important part of setting boundaries and creating balance in your life. But when you're in charge, there is a difference between delegating respectfully and commanding or demanding things of people. This extends beyond your leadership roles and professional life, too. I find that it's most easily explained by using an everyday life example.

Think about this scenario: A person walks into a Starbucks and says, "Give me 5 mocha-locka-choco-spresso-things." It's a command that could have just as easily been said as, "May I please have 5 mocha-locka-choco-spresso drinks?" Or "I would like 5 mocha-locka-choco-spressos, please." The last two examples are simply more respectful. The moral of the story is: If you want to manage expectations well and still keep healthy boundaries... ask, don't task.

When I worked in corporate America, it took me a few years before I truly understood the difference between getting on the phone with a colleague and stating what I needed vs. calling a colleague and first asking if they had five minutes to chat with me. Ultimately, asking instead of tasking creates a win-win for everyone involved, because people feel respected and included in the process. To become a PhD at managing and communicating expectations, respect and inclusion are key. You have a voice. Use it.

When I was younger, I would stay silent. Now? Nope. I can 100% be a team player and help out, but if you're not going to ask me and actually have a conversation about it, I'm going to speak up and create the conversation. Because that's what I'm invested in: the conversation and the connection. Otherwise I'm silently agreeing to someone else's expectations of me, which will only lead to resentment, frustration, and disappointment—for everybody.

Eventually, when that happens, that's when we hit the "emergency" side of expectations. With the desired outcome long past possible, everyone goes into emergency mode to try and "fix" what went wrong. But that ship has already sailed.

It sails away when we decide not to have a (potentially) uncomfortable conversation about expectations. It sails away when we choose to remain silent instead of speaking up and advocating for ourselves. It sails away when we get inflexible about the expectations we hold of others, and it sails away when we hold too high expectations of ourselves.

In short, if you want to embrace the Fuck It! mentality of caring more, you have to be willing to get uncomfortable in order to create more harmony in your relationships and peace within yourself. Say "Fuck It!" and speak up. Say "Fuck It!" and make a filter that helps you focus on what really matters to you. Then say "Fuck It!" and get real with yourself about how you treat yourself when it comes to expectations. I promise it will be worth it.

# Chapter 8

# How Disappointing

If you're 50 or older, you've experienced disappointment in your life somewhere along the way, if not multiple times. It's okay, it's normal. Everyone gets disappointed in their life. Disappointment is common. Nobody escapes it.

Others disappoint us.

We disappoint others.

We disappoint ourselves.

Normal, normal, normal. Disappointment is normal. And frustrating. And disheartening. Or at least it can be. And yet we keep moving forward. As humans, we can be wholeheartedly disappointed in someone or about something, but we still keep going. Sometimes we go back for more disappointment, and sometimes we simply move on. Either way, we keep going. Why?

Because hope is more powerful than disappointment will ever be, and hope is our birthright. We come into the world as an expression of hope on some level, so it's in our DNA. However you want to look at it, whether you're spiritual, religious, non-religious, it doesn't matter. Hope is embedded in who we are, and it's our most natural state of being. So, of course, disappointment is hard. In many ways, disappointment is the antithesis of hope. It's no wonder then that disappointment can often feel bigger than it actually is.

One of the most disappointing things in my life was not having children of my own. I wrote about this earlier in the menopause chapter, and I want to share it again here becuase it's a perfect example of how disappointment can guide you to the wisdom and freedom of a true Fuck It! Firstly, let me say that there were a few times during my marriage when I thought I was pregnant. For those few days or weeks, I nervously smiled inside while simultaneously fearing what it could mean. (Yes, fearing. It seems I had more wisdom than I gave myself credit for at the time.)

In my 30s, I thought a child would "fix" my ex, and I was desperate to have things fixed. Of course, that was incredibly unrealistic on so many levels. Oh, the naiveté of youth!

Today, I couldn't imagine having a kid with my ex. It wouldn't be fair to the kid, actually, as I know that life would be full of one disappointment after another. For me, during our marriage every disappointment was followed by a period of hope, and then another disappointment would pop up and rear its ugly face. All the while, hope played like a soundtrack in the background of my life, prompting me to "try again." I'm all for background music, but I'm much more selective about what I listen to now, and I'd rather be in control of the playlist.

And that's the point.

Disappointment happens most often when we're passively accepting life and not actively pursuing it. So Fuck It!—it's time to start pursuing life!

## Use the stuff!

There's nothing more disappointing in life than regret.

When I was in high school, my parents moved away between my junior and senior years. I ended up finishing school by living with a friend of the family. (Shout out to Shirley!) Then, at the end of my senior year, my friends threw a "going away" party for me. It was epic and a ton of fun. They're still some of my favorite pictures from high school. Everyone gave me gifts and cards, and it was all rather special. One friend, however, made me a collage on a poster. (Shout out to Julie!) I still have it.

Among pictures of me were various phrases and pictures from magazines. At the top of the collage, she had cut out letters that said: "No regrets." This was a phrase of mine from high school, and I'm still somewhat in awe of the younger me when I think about it. Somehow, as a teenager, I knew that regret was a waste of time and energy. Because regret serves no purpose in our lives. Regretting something neither allows you to change it nor learn from it. It's a quicksand emotion, slowly feeding on itself until it takes you under.

No regrets.

As an adult, I think we live with regret far more often than we would like, especially as we get older and start looking backward. Welcome to your 50s! If you want, that can stop now. It's up to you.

There's a book called *The Top Five Regrets of the Dying* in which an Australian nurse, Bronnie Ware, recorded her dying patients' epiphanies when she worked in palliative care. Here's what she observed as the top five regrets people had at the end of their lives (quoted directly):

1. I wish I'd had the courage to live a life true to myself, not the life others expected of me.
2. I wish I hadn't worked so hard.
3. I wish I'd had the courage to express my feelings.
4. I wish I had stayed in touch with my friends.
5. I wish that I had let myself be happier.

Nobody focused on the *things* in their lives, though that is often what we're told to focus on throughout our lives. (Remember: more, more, more!) Instead, every patient focused on the *quality* of their life:

*How* could they have lived differently?
*What* could they have done differently?
*Who* could they have spent more time with?

In my writing career, I spent over a decade (ghost)writing a blog/newsletter for an interiors-based business. The owner of the company offered services from interior design and decorating to move management. As such, she had a lot of senior clients who were rightsizing from the family home to a senior living community. At the end of the day, most of the seniors had trouble parting with a lot of their objects, not because of their monetary value, but because of the *memories* they attached to the object. For them, a small sculpture or piece of art reminded them of a trip with family. A needlepoint cushion reminded them of their mother or sister. The objects were important as far as the memories they triggered.

Nobody regretted giving away the extra chairs or tables. Nobody regretted selling the unused trays and vases in the cabinet. Nobody regretted donating boxes of linens or yard equipment.

However, they *did* regret learning that the precious china, silver, or other items they had kept tucked away for "special occasions" were not as valuable as they thought. The regret was not necessarily because of the monetary value, though that was a harsh realization. No, the regret was for *not having used and enjoyed the items.* Regret also came from learning that nobody in the family wanted them, which possibly happened because they didn't have memories attached to the items since they were rarely used. (See how it comes full circle?)

Regret is about not doing something you wish you had now that you're out of time. So... use the stuff. Use it and enjoy it!

Use the "special" items you save for special occasions and make every day special. Use the china, the silverware, the linens, and the glassware.

Use the handbags and wear the shoes, sweaters, and dresses. With so many people working from home during the Covid pandemic, our ideas about clothing have changed slightly. But you don't need a reason to wear something that makes you feel good other than the fact that it makes you feel good. Wear the sweater.

Use the special blanket and sleep deeply knowing you are surrounded by something you love. Take the time to enjoy the things you have. You will appreciate them more, not less, for using them.

You and your life are reason enough to use these things on a regular basis. (Remember: Celebrate yourself!) Don't look back on your time with disappointment, wishing that you had enjoyed things more.

Yes, they run the risk of getting damaged or breaking completely. Yes, you run the risk of feeling sad when that happens. But you don't break your day-to-day plates, do you? You don't damage your everyday mugs or shoes. So why do you think you will damage the "special" ones?

I am 100% guilty of this.

I have things that I kept simply because I love them. (Remember, I was a fashion buyer.) I have all these nice things, and for years, I didn't use them. Most of them have sat in boxes or storage for the last 15 years since I left the fashion industry. Yes, some have come out for special occasions, such as the holidays, but for the most part, I have kept everything nicely tucked away.

Everything was tucked away until one day in my 47th year when I said, *"Fuck it! I'm using it, and I'm going to enjoy it!"*

Life is meant to be enjoyed. Yes, it can also be hard, and we can have struggles. Perhaps that's even *more* reason to enjoy the things you love. And here's a pro tip: If you don't love it, get rid of it. Sell it, donate it, or give it to a friend or family member who would enjoy it. I have a friend who taught me this phrase: "Let it be a blessing to someone else." If you don't like something, let it go and stop giving it real estate in your mind and your space.

I know it's not always easy to let go of something you think you *should* want or keep. When I walked out of my marriage, I had three days to pack up and leave. I didn't want him to fight my divorce request, so I left with only that which was mine. This meant that, other than my personal belongings, I left the house almost entirely intact except for the wedding gifts that had been from my side, with one exception: the china.

I hated our china.

Well, maybe "hate" is a strong word, but I really disliked it. I didn't choose it, he did. It was pretty enough, and simple enough to go with anything or be used for any occasion, but I rarely took it out because I simply didn't like it. So when it came time to divide that stuff up, I decided to keep what I picked out (the crystal—which is gorgeous!) and leave what he picked out.

Ultimately, my ex requested two place settings of the crystal, and I agreed, simply to get him to sign the papers so I could move on. It's a decision I don't regret at all. Any of it. I walked away from a bad situation, and I was able to let go of the china in the process. I didn't enjoy it, I wasn't going to use it, so it made no sense to keep it.

If I loved it, I imagine it would have been more difficult to walk away from, and perhaps I would have divided things differently. It all comes back to what you like—or better yet, love.

If you love something—use it. Have your morning tea or coffee in a beautiful cup and saucer with a lovely piece of toast beside it on a beautiful plate. Wear the soft sweater you keep tucked away and enjoy the feeling of warmth it gives you. Have fun spotting your reflection in a passing mirror or pane of glass as you spy yourself wearing the earrings you save for special occasions.

Figure out where you're "saving something for a special occasion," and make that occasion your life! You are more than worth it. I promise.

## Do or don't

The Fuck It! Lifestyle states that in your day-to-day life, you get to decide what makes you happy. You're 50 now. If you can't do it now, when are you ever going to be able to?

Don't like wearing heels? Fuck It! Don't wear them.

Don't like doing pilates or running? Fuck It! Don't do either.

Don't like eating kale? Fuck It! Don't eat kale.

Do you like long walks? Fuck It! Take the walk.

Do you like pickled herring? Fuck It! Buy it and enjoy!

Do you like wearing athleisure? Fuck It! You do you, boo.

When you really sit down and evaluate it, there are very few things in life where we *have* to conform or be a certain way. Job descriptions, for example, are not typically negotiated, so dress codes for work are usually something you can't just say Fuck It! to.

Similarly, there's common courtesy to be considered in life. Nobody likes sitting next to someone who is eating boiled eggs on a plane. I'm all for upping your protein, but please don't do this. I once sat next to a woman who thought it was okay to paint her nails. (Seriously, don't be that person.) This was before the liquid ban on planes, so I'm just grateful that she didn't also bring nail polish remover. Yikes!

Ultimately, you're going to have disappointments in life. This is inescapable. What's avoidable, however, is whether you play a role in them or not. If you have a role in your disappointment, then you can say Fuck It! and change whatever it was that you did so that you have less disappointment in the future. Ta-daaa! It's Fuck It! Magic.

## Chapter 9

# Everybody Hurts

I'm a child of the 70s and 80s (hence: 50). This makes me a proud member of Generation X. We are the generation of self-reliance and pop music. (I like to think we're the "middle child" of the larger "generations" family. I mean, it's pretty obvious that the Boomers are the first child, right?) As such, I think we learned to express life through lyrics.

In almost every stage of my life since I was nine years old, I have collected quotes. Initially it was all music quotes, but eventually I layered on writing quotes. I had a quote book—okay, I had several—in which I would write down the words that outwardly expressed what I was feeling inside. As a writer, I think it's fascinating that most of my inspiration when I was younger came from other people's words.

So when it came time to write this chapter, I borrowed from R.E.M. (one of the most notable bands of the 80s) who wrote *Everybody Hurts*. I'll share a portion of the lyrics[1] here:

> *When your day is long*
> *And the night, the night is yours alone*
> *When you're sure you've had enough*
> *Of this life, well hang on*

---

1 All lyrics are property and copyright of their respective authors, artists, and labels.

*Don't let yourself go*
*'Cause everybody cries*
*Everybody hurts sometimes*

*...*

*If you're on your own in this life*
*The days and nights are long*
*When you think you've had too much*
*Of this life to hang on*

*Well, everybody hurts sometimes*
*Everybody cries*
*Everybody hurts, sometimes*

It's a pretty simple message, isn't it? Everybody hurts (you're "normal"), so you're not alone (even though it might feel like you are), so hang on (this hurt is temporary, allow it to pass, it will get better). Hold on.

Well, you're 50 now, which means "hurt" is potentially going to be part of your new normal. We've already briefly touched on the physical aches and pains that seem to come with growing older. While I don't believe it's a certainty that we will all have aches and pains (or that we necessarily need to subscribe to that idea), I do believe that a lot of our physical body parts have lifespans. Much like tires on your car, things wear down over time and use. When they're replenished naturally, it's fine. But when the replenishment slows down (as can happen with aging), the wear and tear becomes more noticeable. Hence... pain. Something I hear a lot of my 50-something friends now including in regular conversation.

The "hurt" we don't talk as readily about when we enter our fifth decade of life is the emotional pain that sometimes comes with being 50. All of a sudden, we're at an age where our parents might be ailing or dying, and our friends' parents are doing the same. It's like,

"Welcome to your 50s... people you know are going to start dying now." *Sigh*.

Death is a part of life, oddly enough. And yet, like menopause, we don't talk about it. At least not in the West. For a long time, I have secretly admired other cultures and how they deal with death. Watching BBC World News as they share a film from somewhere halfway around the world of women wailing at the death of a loved one always filled me with envy. Odd, I know. While I saw sadness on the screen, I also saw freedom. Freedom to express yourself without regard for what others were thinking. The notion of "keeping a stiff upper lip" simply doesn't exist in a moment of loss like that.

For years I watched this and admired their ability to let go and freely allow their emotions to flow. I mean, death is sad, and loss is hard. When they're combined, it can be overwhelming to the system. So why not let it out in such an epic way?

Well, I did.

Possibly as the precursor to "50 and Fuck It!"—or as the catalyst for it—when I was four months shy of my 49th birthday, my father passed away. After more than 14 years of being disabled by a massive stroke, his body finally succumbed to an infection. I say "finally" because I lost track of the number of times during the previous decade and a half in which we thought he might be passing. When you live with the possibility of death almost every day, life gets a bit warped, or at least your perception of it does.

Actually, though, I think life gets a lot clearer, and you realize that your perception beforehand was what was warped. There's bliss in the ignorance of death or dying. So even though we expected him to die, I didn't allow myself to *really* expect it. Nor did I expect my response.

My mom came to my room around 10:30 p.m. that evening to tell me that they had called from the care home to give us the news. Thankfully, we had been able to see him during the day and a half prior as his condition worsened from the infection. Even with the pandemic, the care home knew the importance of allowing tightly controlled visits when someone was on the verge of passing (not from Covid). I will be forever grateful to them for that.

After Mom and I hugged, the only thing to do was go to bed. Everything had been taken care of for us, as we had set it all up in advance. (Another aspect of life that nobody tells you about, but was "normal" for us, was doing all the advance planning for death. If you haven't done this with your parents, please consider it. You will be glad you did.)

I went to bed and had a half-sleep for about six hours. Around 7 a.m., I got up, got dressed, and left the house. I went to the beach even though it was October and it was cold, and I talked to my brother and then my godfather on the phone. I was crying, I was sad, and I was trying to hold it (somewhat) together. My friend, Patty, showed up at the beach with tea and something to eat. I don't remember if I ate or not, but the tea was very welcome. We spent an hour or more in the car at the beach intermittently talking and crying.

When I finally felt like I could pull myself together, I returned home. At which point I realized I had grief coursing through my veins, and the images of the women halfway around the world hit me. I ran out the back door, fell to my knees on the grass, and sobbed. I sobbed, and wailed, and cried until my body was exhausted and probably dehydrated. Patty came outside with me and simply rubbed my back. Unfortunately, she knew the pain of losing a parent, too. Wailing was the best thing I could have done.

Crying in this uncontrolled way, as it turns out, is healthy. Or at least it was healthy for me. Being able to pour myself out all at one time is ultimately what gave me breath. It gave me much-needed space. There's no shame in sobbing, not for me. Not anymore. The notion that I should withhold my sadness for someone else's comfort—or to prevent their discomfort—is something I can't support any longer.

And that's the crux of it, isn't it?

By the time we're 50, we have spent the better part of four or five decades engaging with life in ways that prevent someone else's discomfort. We apologize, shrink, and diminish ourselves because we think—or we're told—it's the right thing to do. It's considerate. It's nice. It may be thoughtful. But is it kind? I have a friend who has two daughters, and she once told me that she has been teaching them: Don't be "nice"—be kind.

There's a difference between being "nice" and being kind. Kindness is universal, and it's born of something deep within. Being "nice," on the other hand, is usually based on external expectations, ideals, and pressures. While you may think it's nice to hide your emotions from others so that they don't feel uncomfortable, it's actually unkind to you. It would be kind for others to allow you to feel what you're feeling and simply hold space for you as you do.

After all, everybody hurts.

Everybody knows what it feels like to feel pain of some sort. How amazing would it be if we allowed ourselves and others the freedom to express it... knowing we aren't alone.

## Chapter 10

# Eat the Damn Cake!

Now we're going to get into possibly the most divisive topic in the whole book: food!

More specifically... ketchup on scrambled eggs.

You probably either nodded with that statement or wanted to gag a little bit. If you were in the middle and felt neutral, you are in the minority. This is one of those subjects that I have found to be instantly divisive. Another example is mayonnaise on French fries.

Yeah, that's what I said. Mayonnaise. On. French fries. Yum!

You either love it or hate it. Just like you either love ketchup on your scrambled eggs or you don't.

People are passionate about their food, and they're even more passionate about their cultural identity when it comes to food. In short, we eat what we know, or what we were taught to eat.

When I was growing up, I lived in a somewhat divided household when it came to food. My father was American of Irish descent on both sides, and my mother is Venezuelan of Venezuelan and Dutch descent. So growing up, I was always fascinated by what other people ate in their homes, especially my friends. For the most part, I only got sugared cereal when I went to sleep at a friend's house. My mom's version of sugary cereal was either a bowl of plain cheerios or that ginormous brick of shredded wheat, over which she'd let us sprinkle a teaspoon of sugar.

Additionally, we rarely had any chips or soda in our house, but if we did, it was usually the original Doritos because Mom liked them. Or the little potato sticks because she liked those, too. Junk food just wasn't often a part of our pantry. (Those little potato sticks are awesome, by the way! She still eats them and now I do, too.)

For the most part, I remember my mom focusing on giving us a really balanced diet. For example, she believed in the "once a week" method for protein.

Once a week we had chicken.

Once a week we had beef.

Once a week we had pork.

Once a week we had fish.

Once a week we had organ meat, like liver.

This was, of course, for dinner, and I don't remember what filled the remaining two days, but it was probably chicken again or a meatless night. Accompanying these meats, Mom alternated between white rice and mashed potatoes, with either broccoli, green beans, asparagus, or peas on the side. We also almost always had salad. And to drink? Milk or water. Occasionally, we had apple juice. There wasn't a lot of bread, if any, and the condiments we enjoyed with dinner were typically mayonnaise and Mom's homemade red wine vinaigrette salad dressing. (Which is delicious!)

Having been raised in another country with a totally different cultural palette, Mom focused on mastering a set rotation of dishes that aligned with a more American menu. Occasionally, she would make us a dish or two from her roots in Venezuela, such as: ropa vieja, arroz con pollo, or picadillo. (If you haven't tried any of these dishes, do yourself a favor and find them somewhere. And arepas. You can thank me later.)

All in all, it may sound like we were uber healthy. Interestingly, however, as I have learned more about health and nutrition as an adult, I realize how limited the produce aspect was. Fruit wasn't a big part of our diet. Mom made sure we had the basics, such as apples, bananas, oranges, or grapes (and in the summer months—raspberries!), but it pretty much stopped there. I don't remember having a lot of different fruits growing up. I don't remember them being available in the grocery store, actually. I *do* remember, however, that my mom had to cajole me into eating bananas regularly by smothering them in chocolate sauce! (I still don't eat bananas, even with chocolate sauce.)

Beyond making food more enticing with teaspoons of sugar and bowlfuls of liquid chocolate, my parents also encouraged us to try things as children. We didn't have to like them or eat them, but we had to try them. Some of the things I tried included:

Snails and periwinkles

Dandelion salad

Venison (deer)

Frogs' legs

Chicken feet

Tongue

(The only ones I liked were the snails—but really I just liked the garlic-parsley butter they were cooked in and the French bread used to sop it all up.)

Additionally, though I didn't think it odd or weird as a kid, I can look back on some of the things I enjoyed or ate and realize they're not necessarily part of the "norm" for today's kids. Olives, cornichons, and pickles (apparently I liked briny foods) were a definite favorite growing up. I remember my American grandparents started every dinner with a designated plate of celery stalks, olives, and a small glass of tomato juice. I feel like nuts were involved, too, but I don't remember for sure.

Considering all this, it should come as no surprise that I have an "interesting" relationship with food. It's from this perspective that I worked on completely changing things in my 40s, and how turning 50 has allowed me to say Fuck It! when it comes to food.

Back to ketchup on scrambled eggs.

## Ketchup on scrambled eggs

My paternal grandparents were the ones who introduced me to this combo. It grossed my mother out to no end, and still does. I have no recollection of what my father or my siblings thought of it, though. I only remember my mom's reaction, probably because I actually liked the combo (and still do), and her reaction was not subtle. I remember seeing her grimace as she spontaneously and loudly said, "That's disgusting!" with a gutteral sound of disgust in her tone.

For me, there's something about the sweet and slightly salty flavor of ketchup that bounces really well off the taste and texture of the scrambled eggs. Mind you, I only like this with scrambled eggs—no other egg preparation seems to work for me. For a couple of years, I switched to salsa instead of ketchup, especially when I lived in Texas, but for the most part, I still like a little bit of ketchup with my scrambled eggs.

For years, however, I hid my affinity for this combo out of fear and shame. I didn't want others to think I was gross or disgusting in how I ate. I also didn't want to appear "unsophisticated" in some way. After all, ketchup is not necessarily considered an ingredient in "fine dining" (though it was the main ingredient in my dad's homemade barbecue sauce). I would only add ketchup to my plate if I could guarantee I'd be alone. Even as I write this, I want to diminish it slightly by assuring you that I don't pour the ketchup all over the eggs, but rather I have a little bit on the side that I dip my eggs into.

But no more. I'm tired of hiding the things I enjoy, and now that I'm 50, I can say Fuck It! and enjoy them. If you don't like it, you don't have to do it. I'm not asking anyone else to put ketchup on their scrambled eggs. I simply want to enjoy the things I like—so I'm going to.

I think this is what's important.

Especially as women, we are told all the time what we *should* eat, or *should* like to eat. People stare at me quizzically when I say I don't like bananas. In fact, I often get the response, "What do you mean you *don't like bananas*?!" And when I say I don't like banana bread, I get: "How can you *not* like banana bread?! It's banana bread!"

I get it. It's delicious, right? How can I not like something that almost everyone I meet thinks is amazing?

Because I don't.

It's that simple.

More importantly, it *can* be that simple.

If you like something, eat it. If you don't like something, don't eat it. Don't like kale? Fuck It! Don't eat it. (Yes, I've mentioned kale twice now. I know.)

Don't like mayonnaise or mustard? Fuck It! Don't use them.

Don't like milk? Or tea? Or coffee? Fuck It! Don't drink them.

That's another one of the more fascinating conversations I have with people who often stare at me in disbelief as a response. I don't like coffee. I never have. I spent one summer during my college years in which I drank coffee and enjoyed it. I lived in Spain, and the coffee was delicious—provided I added cream and sugar. So it's probably more accurate to say that I liked melted coffee ice cream, warmed up. (Though I think it also had something to do with the actual coffee in Spain, as it wasn't bitter at all.)

I like tea. I always have. My father was a tea drinker, and I grew up watching him have English Breakfast tea each morning with a splash of milk. When I was younger, I thought it was disgusting that he didn't add sugar. But now? Now I enjoy my Irish breakfast tea every morning with milk, no sugar. It's delicious.

If you like something, you are 100% allowed to enjoy it without apologizing or making excuses or offering reasons for why you like it. You are the only person you have to be concerned about when it comes to food. So go ahead and put the ketchup on the scrambled eggs. Or salsa. Or whatever it is that makes you happy. Because eating is not meant to be as difficult as we seem to make it.

## You can dance if you want to, you can leave your friends behind...

You get to eat what you like, and you get to not eat what you don't like. While there are some things you may want to consider, such as nutritional value, calories, and timing, you get to decide what you eat. Every day. You do you, boo.

You *can* eat the damn cake, if you want to. And if you don't want to, you can decline it. This isn't *Fear Factor*. It is incredibly rare to be in a situation where you *have* to eat something. In those circumstances, there are polite ways to decline or redirect. And if you really have to eat it? Do what I did growing up:

- Find your favorite condiment (or any condiment available to you) and smother it.
- Pinch your nose as you chew, then swallow in one gulp. (This works, though it wasn't as effective as I would have hoped for the colonoscopy liquid.)
- Shoot it back like a shot of hard liquor, and then chase it with a beverage.
- Hide it in your napkin or shoes.

Yes, I actually did that last one.

One time my mom made an angel food cake for someone and frosted it with chocolate icing. I thought I would be really clever and pick a couple of bites from the inside by sticking my tiny kid hand down the hole in the center. I figured nobody would notice. Apparently, however, there is a limit to how many times you can go back and remove the inside of a cake before it falls in on itself. This was not something I thought about as a kid (because... angel food cake). My mom got so mad at me for messing up her cake that my punishment was to eat the rest of the cake... all by myself without leaving the table. Really? This was a reward, not a punishment! Or at least you'd think so, wouldn't you? Indeed, I thought the same at the time.

I was wrong.

As it turns out, it's not easy to eat an entire cake in one sitting. Even though as kids, we imagine that we can, I'm here to say that it's pretty hard. In fact, it will probably make you ill, as it did for me. So once I started to feel like I couldn't eat anymore, when my mom wasn't looking, I stuffed pieces of the cake in my shoes. Thankfully, angel food cake compresses *really* well! I managed to fill both shoes and still get my feet inside just enough to hobble to the bathroom, where I promptly emptied my shoes into the toilet and flushed the cake away.

I think I took two or three trips to the bathroom before my mom finally released me from the table with about a quarter of the cake left. I should probably ask her if she ever knew that I did that with my shoes. I can honestly say that I never tried to sneakily pick at a cake again, though I also feel like I could do it better now, knowing that you can only get away with so much before it loses its internal support and collapses.

The same goes for most food, actually. It's all about enjoying what you like and doing it in a way that supports you. If you eat only one thing—especially in excess—things will probably collapse. Over the years, I've learned that I like a lot more fruit and vegetables than I ever thought I would growing up, but that doesn't mean that I want to eat all of them every day. I couldn't. My body would collapse.

(And then the toilet would probably collapse with all that fiber! TMI? Sorry.) Nor do I want to eat just one of them all the time. That would be tedious and boring.

Instead, I focus on enjoying what I enjoy, and I say Fuck It! to the rest. More importantly, my relationship with food has changed. I see it as both something to enjoy and something that fuels and supports my body. As I age, I lean more into the support side of things, too, as I want to be old *and* healthy. I want to be able to enjoy my life for many years to come, especially now that I've found Fuck It! Freedom. I still won't eat bananas, no matter how "healthy" they are for me because I don't like them. Can't even be around the smell. So I choose not to, and I hope you can do the same.

I hope you can say Fuck It! and say no to the things you don't like while saying yes to what you love, what supports you, and what tastes good and makes you feel good.

## Chapter 11

# No Shirt, No Shoes, No Problem!

How many times in your life have you heard some variation of, "You shouldn't wear that," either directly or indirectly? If you're 50, it's probably been a lot—especially indirectly.

Women, in general, have been told what to wear, when, and how for most of their lives. While I agree that there are certain occasions when a dress code needs to be adhered to (you may not want to wear a sarong and tee shirt to a black tie wedding, perhaps, or maybe you do... I don't know), in our daily lives, there are very few clothing "rules" we need to observe.

During my college years, I spent one summer working at a law firm in Houston, Texas. Yes, Texas. In the summer. It was Hot with a capital H! And it was swampy. Houston in the summer has the kind of weather that makes you want to shower several times a day. At the very least, it makes you appreciate a cold(er) shower. So when I went to work at this law firm, I was shocked to learn that women had to wear pantyhose if they wore a skirt or a dress, and anything sleeveless was off-limits.

While I understand the need to set rules around dressing professionally, it was a bit of a burden to wear pantyhose in 110° heat with 99% humidity. If you've ever sweated from your calves before, you'll know what I mean. I regularly found myself blasting my car's air conditioning on my feet and legs in order to dry up the sweat that had formed as a thin layer between my skin and its nylon encasement during the brief walk between my house and my car, which was approximately 20 feet!

Of course, it didn't matter, because once I parked my car in the outdoor parking lot by the office building, I then had to walk a block and a half in the same heat and develop a new layer of sweat underneath my legs' silky cage.

Thankfully, everything in Houston is air conditioned, so it didn't take long for it all to dry up again. It also didn't take long to begin to freeze during the day while inside the building. This meant that a lunch outing became more than just a quest for food; it actually served to warm you up! I learned very quickly that layers were an essential aspect of dressing professionally for work in Houston, and I invested in an array of cotton cardigans as a result.

But this idea that "you can't or shouldn't" wear something isn't really about work attire or dress codes. Private businesses and other organizations do have a right to create standards for how their employees dress. In fact, it's often helpful to the employee to know what's acceptable and what's not. It makes getting dressed in the morning, or clothes shopping, much easier in the long run.

Personally, I loved having a uniform growing up. While I participated in the obligatory complaining about having to wear one, I recognize that it made my life a lot easier when it came to getting ready in the morning. My previously described lengthy school day didn't include extra time in the morning for changing outfits or wondering what to wear. Once I was in high school, I could get dressed in under five minutes. Sometimes less!

A uniform is one thing, dress codes are another, and both are understandable given the circumstances and environment. What's not understandable, however, are societal pressures to look and dress a certain way, especially when it's based on some arbitrary and antiquated rule, or even worse... your size, gender, or age.

## Black and blue and plaid all over

"Don't wear white after Labor Day or before Memorial Day."

"Don't show your midriff (if it isn't flat)."

"Don't mix patterns."

"Don't wear pink and red together."

"Don't wear blue and black together."

"Don't mix metals in your jewelry."

"Don't wear heels to a garden party." (Well, if they're thin and pointy, that one is just smart.)

Don't, don't, don't, don't... don't. "Don't" has replaced "should" when it comes to most of the rules about dressing. And these aren't even the rules related to age! What I've written above is just a sample of the things I remember hearing throughout my life. Of course, there were many more "rules" about what to wear, including: colors or patterns (specifically based on body size) as well as hem length, neck length, and arm length of any particular garment. Many of these "rules" seem to align a bit more with chronological age than anything else.

If you're 50 or older (which presumably you are, or close to, if you're reading this book), you know some of the rules I am referring to and have seen these lists. If you're under 50, you've still probably heard many of them throughout your life and know what I'm referring to. It often looks like this:

**Women of a certain age shouldn't wear:**
**_____ (fill in the blank).**

*Sigh.* Growing up in the 70s and 80s, I was told that a girl shouldn't wear black until she's 16, and not just by my parents. This seemed to be one of those arbitrary holdovers from a time gone by when black clothing was intended to mean mourning. While this may be a personal preference, it's not based on any sort of sound argument. (None of this is, actually.) I mean, how cute is a five year old in a pretty black velvet dress with a lace collar during the holidays? Presumably just as cute as a five year old in a red velvet dress, a plaid dress, or any other color dress. Or pants. Or a skirt. Five year olds are just cute, especially when they get dressed up! Does it really matter what color they're wearing? Or style? Or pattern?

For that matter, does it really matter what we wear?

No, not really. Yet a lot of people seem to get easily bothered by what other people are wearing.

Want to know what *does* matter?

How. You. Feel.

How you feel in what you're wearing—whatever it is—is what matters most. Nobody has to "like" what you're wearing except you. Phew! What a relief, right?

If only it were that easy.

Unfortunately, decades of conditioning might make this a bit harder for many of us. I know that for me, I still have a few hang ups about what I'm wearing and whether it's "right" or not.

Especially as a plus-size woman, navigating the "shoulds" of fashion can be incredibly challenging. Not to mention: demoralizing, disappointing, frustrating, heart-breaking, aggravating, and often unfair and financially impactful. (Did you know plus-size fashion is often more expensive? I get it. It costs more in raw materials, but still, it's frustrating to see because it isn't applied evenly across the board. My smaller shoe size isn't less expensive, for example.)

Personally, there are many "styles" I look at and admire on other women that I simply can't embrace with my body the way it currently is. Even when I wasn't plus-size, I was still very curvy. I've always had an hourglass silhouette of some sort.

I'm also short, so I couldn't wear the droopy silhouettes that look incredibly comfy while still remaining polished-looking. Think: wide-legged linen pants and flowing tunics with a long necklace. Of course, this didn't stop me from trying the look. (I did say it was comfy!) But once I had everything on, it just made me look even shorter and wider, which I didn't want.

And that is the key to all of this.

I used the word "I" in that sentence: *I didn't want it.* Me. Not society, not a family member, not a partner... me.

I have since purchased (and worn) numerous pairs of wide-legged trousers because I love them. I also wear "skinny" trousers, bootleg jeans, and bottoms of all shapes. Some days I feel particularly happy in leggings. Other days you won't get me near a pair. Some days I wear tunics and long sweaters, and other days I wear blouses slightly tucked into whatever I have going on below. It all depends on my mood and what I have happening that day.

The pandemic definitely caused me to expand on my options for comfy clothing, as long days on the computer for writing, editing, or repeated virtual meetings required a lack of a firm waistband. So jeans and similar clothing were relegated to the back of the closet while yoga-style pants (with pockets!) became a staple. It's all about what you *like,* both in how it looks and how it feels.

The same goes for color.

I can't tell you how many times I've worn white after Labor Day, and not a "winter white," either. I also remember the first time I paired navy blue with black, I had to pause. I was taught that you don't do that. And yet I really loved the look. It has since become a staple. I also wear pink with red or orange, and black in all of its spectrum. I have a closet with plaids, florals, paisleys, and solids, though I don't really wear stripes.

I actually love the look of a classic striped blue and white shirt or sweater. So much so that I continue to buy striped clothing. And then

I put it on. Every time I do this and walk past a mirror, I don't like it. For me, stripes don't work. So I don't wear stripes, and I think I'm finally at the point of not buying them ever again. Thankfully, I love donating clothing to worthy charities. All my discards go specifically to help women in need.

Over the years, I have learned to donate clothing twice a year, every time I change my closet from summer to winter and vice versa. This process has helped me really hone in on what I like and what I don't like. For example, I have a favorite blouse from the late 90s that I will never give away. Similarly, I have certain styles of clothing that I know work well with my body and make me happy when I wear them. They make getting dressed effortless. I keep all of those. (Yes, even if I haven't worn them in the past year. Fuck It, Konmari!)

The bottom line is that the only "rule" that you need to adhere to in what you wear is this: Do you like it?

If you like it, Fuck It! and wear what you want.

Do you like wearing plaids? Fuck It! and enjoy them.

Do you like wearing stripes or florals? Fuck It! and wear *all* the flowers.

Do you like wearing black? Or yellow? Or greige? Fuck It! and wear the greige!

Nobody can tell you what you like, only you can do that. And if you forget what that feels like, watch a five year old dress themselves. They choose the things that make them happy. This is how we get the unicorn-loving, cowboy-mermaid-princess-ballerinas that walk around the grocery store with confidence in all their colorful tutu glory. Thank God!

## Long hair don't care

I can sense myself wanting to burst into song as I type that. I directed the musical *HAIR* when I was in college, and now the lyrics are on repeat in my head: *"Gimme a head with hair, Long, beautiful heh-air!...*" but I digress. Back to being ourselves in a world that tries to get us to conform.

As women in the Western hemisphere, another area in which we are expected to comply with some sort of (Western) standard of appearance is with our hair. As we get older, it is somehow expected that our hair will get shorter—or *should* get shorter (and puffier!). While there are some practicalities to shorter hair, it's not a foregone conclusion that you need to go that route as you age. If you want to, great! It can certainly be easier at times.

Where hair is concerned, it isn't just about aging. If you had short hair when you were younger, I bet you experienced some pressure to grow it out along the way. I know I had friends who did. It sounded something like, "She would be so much prettier if she just let her hair grow out a little more." *Sigh.*

One of the things that I admired about Queen Elizabeth II was her hairstyle. If you look back at photos of her throughout her life, it's almost as if she stumbled upon a style that she really liked in her 20s and simply decided that was what she would have for the rest of her life. Done and done. Certainly makes getting ready a lot easier, doesn't it? While I don't know for sure, I am assuming that she liked her hair that way, which is why she never changed it. If so, good for her!

Now you have to answer the questions. Do you like your hair? Do you not like your hair? Are you unsure what you want? The easiest way to answer these questions is to do what I did: Change it! Change your hair and see what happens.

When I cut my hair to the length of an above-the-shoulder/below-the-ear bob, I looked like a bobblehead! My face is fairly round regardless of how much I weigh, so, naturally, a bob made my face look more circular. While it was somewhat cute for a little while, I hated it. I didn't find it easier to maintain. In fact, it was a lot more maintenance than my traditional long locks that I often throw up into a ponytail. Not only that, but it made me realize that I have a natural wave or curl to my hair that is more pronounced when short. It became much more annoying to have to try and straighten in order to keep the uniform "bob" look.

Speaking of high-maintenance looks, I also tried dyeing my hair chocolate brown. Yes. Yes, I did.

It's probably the half-Irish in me, but there's something captivating about a woman with dark hair and blue eyes. So I tried it. Every time I walked by a mirror, it had an unexpected effect. With dark brown hair, I didn't hate what I saw. I couldn't—because I didn't know who I was looking at! Whenever I spied myself, I saw a stranger. It wasn't me. It would literally take a long pause for me to realize it was me looking back. Needless to say, the chocolate hair didn't last. However, I have since tried adding purple extensions now and then, just for fun, and that has been great! If the actual clips holding them in place weren't so annoying, I'd probably do it more often. (My next adventure will be to tie single strands of glitter into my hair!)

Speaking of hair color, if you've gone grey *up* there, you're probably also going grey *down* there... and *under* there, too (talking about the armpits, here). I recently saw a friend's post on Facebook that read: "Is it possible to dye your pubes? Asking for a friend." I laughed outright. It's hair, so it probably is. Personally, I already find it a bit of a burden to manage the increasingly grey situation going on on top of my head on a semi-regular basis. (But hear me when I say that I *want* to, which is why I do it—not because I *should* or I'm supposed to.) Therefore, the last thing I would want to do is add another layer of color-related hair dyeing maintenance! But as the saying goes: You do you, boo! If you want to dye your pubes, have at it! Just please, if you do, let me know how it went (because you know we all want to know).

Knowing what you like—and what you don't like—is what matters. Maybe you're someone who likes changing things up regularly. Fuck It! Have at it and have fun! Or maybe you're like the Queen and you only want one style for everything because you love it or it's easier... or both. Fuck It! You do you, boo.

Part of standing in our boots involves giving ourselves the space and time to really know who we are from the inside out. Once we do that, it becomes a lot easier to make the choices that align with that person. As a result, we end up presenting ourselves to the outside world in a much more powerful way.

When you wear what you love and look the way you love, you can't help but feel good about yourself and your life. That translates to everything else in your world. So if you love skirts and dresses, Fuck It! and embrace them. Wear them everywhere, for everything. If you hate skirts and dresses, then remove them from your closet. Give them away and let them be a blessing to somebody else.

"You can't wear that" is not part of the Fuck It! Lifestyle. What is part of embracing "50 and Fuck It!" is knowing that you can wear what makes you happy, whether it's clothing, shoes, a hairstyle, or anything in between. You do you, boo. Pull out those boots, put them on, and stand up!

# Chapter 12

# Knowing Yourself

I was talking with a fellow author and energy worker a while ago, and in the middle of our conversation, I said, "You can't 'Om' your life away." She laughed and said, "I love that!" We then had a really good conversation about what it means to be in balance, as I shared that this was a phrase I have used for over a decade with many of my clients in order to explain "balance" in a new way.

When people come to work with me, they are often looking for a quick fix (thank you, Culture of Do), or they have done years of different therapies and are exhausted. Either way, they often think that if they just meditated/slept/worked/read/did/understood/exercised *more,* they'd be better. (There it is again: more, more, more!)

None of this is true, however, because the "intervention of more" is just a distraction from the actual work that needs to be done. More meditating won't fix the chronic imbalance in your gut, just as more exercise won't help you heal the emotional trauma from your childhood. You can't "Om" your issues away... which is to say you can't do one thing to excess and expect to have the results you desire.

Another way to look at it is this: The intervention must match the dysfunction. An emotional symptom needs an emotional solution.

A physical symptom needs a physical solution. And on and on. While you can sometimes use something different to stimulate a reaction, such as a physical experience to stimulate an emotional reaction, the solution will always need to be aligned with the issue.

By 50, my hope is that you want to know yourself better. I mean, Fuck It! It's time, right? Who are you? Who do you want to be? Who did you leave behind when life seemed to take over... everything? What matters to you? What do you want to do with your days? Your hours? Your minutes? If you don't know yourself, how are you ever going to answer any of these questions?

Remember how I mentioned my favorite cake in Chapter 2? What's your favorite cake? Or your favorite dessert? Do you have one? Could you answer what you'd want for your last meal, if you had to? What about music? Or movies? So much of our life is filled with external stimuli that we've completely disconnected from ourselves and forgotten who we are.

There's a fun exercise in a grocery store that I give my clients to help them start to reconnect to their true self. Personally, I enjoy grocery shopping, but the exercise is pretty simple, even if you don't. Go into a grocery store and walk slowly through the produce section. Pause in front of each item and simply notice your thoughts and feelings. Get curious. That's all. We're so accustomed to going to the store and buying the same five items that we make a bee line past everything else. We're also so over-programmed that our time to shop is incredibly limited, which also forces us to rush through and just "grab what we need" without ever stopping to think about whether it's something we actually *want*.

This is how I learned that I actually like oranges and don't particularly like kiwi. I mean, kiwi is fine, but it's not an orange! I also learned that I don't like oranges when they're not in season. They get drier, smaller, and have significantly less flavor and juiciness. So in the summer months, when you'd think they'd be refreshing on a hot day, I don't want them because they're not as delicious as they are in the winter months.

Knowing yourself is how you can really begin to embrace the Fuck It! Lifestyle. If you know yourself, you stop making excuses and apologizing. You live more proactively and intentionally, with balance, love, and inner peace. (Yes, it's 100% possible.)

## Swinging on a see-saw

"Balance" is one of those buzzwords we hear often in the wellness industry. The biggie, of course, is "work-life balance." I recently saw a quote by Sheryl Sandberg (former[2] COO of Meta, aka: Facebook, etc): *There is no such thing as work-life balance. There's work, and there's life, and there's no balance.* Ouch.

No balance? I beg to differ.

Balance comes from understanding three very simple things:

1. Life has four primary aspects of health.
2. Life is a spiral cycle, not a circular one.
3. Life is multifaceted.

I'd like to add a fourth aspect to balance now that I'm 50, but we'll get to that in a bit. For now, let's focus on this game of life that can sometimes make you feel like you're swinging on a see-saw.

To start with, there are four aspects to health. While we used to think it was only two (mind-body) before it became three (mind-body-soul), it's now commonly looked at as four: physical, mental, emotional, and spiritual.

When I first started studying the etheric arts, such as Reiki, I thought I could fix all my problems by simply doing energy work on everything. I thought that if I meditated extensively, everything would balance itself naturally. It doesn't. (Remember, you can't "Om" your life away.) Similarly, I have had clients (and know others) who have

---

2 She stepped down in August 2022 .

tried the approach of exercising excessively every day to restore balance to their health. That doesn't work either.

In order to have balance with our health, we have to balance out the four aspects. This means that our physical health is equally as important as our mental health, our emotional health, and our spiritual health. It does not mean that if you have 16 waking hours in your day, you need to spend four hours on each. It means that you need to consider each aspect, cumulatively, throughout your days, weeks, months, and years. Recognizing this broader perspective is key to creating a state of balance and getting off the proverbial see-saw.

Similarly, our lives are a spiral, not a circle. This means that when you feel as though you've come back around to the same spot, you haven't. Though it may feel the same, it's often a level or two up from the last time you felt this way. You are, in essence, moving along a spiral which creates a sense of familiarity each time you come back around to a certain point or experience, but time and growth give you a different perspective. Recognizing that "familiarity" doesn't mean "same" is key to getting off the proverbial swing and creating opportunity for more balance.

And now that you're off both the swing and see-saw, balance is yours as long as you acknowledge that life is multifaceted. Sheryl Sandberg's quote separates out life from work, and that's the problem. Work is (for most of us) part of life. It's not separate. By acknowledging that life has numerous and varied aspects to it we can embrace the notion of balance more easily through points one and two. Then, as the compassionate people we are, we can also recognize that we don't all have the same aspects, which allows us to be more supportive of both ourselves and others. Win-win!

## Greet yourself

When I was younger, I used to think I had to be everything to everybody. I used to call myself a chameleon, of sorts, because I adapted to what the person in front of me needed. Nowadays, that's called codependence, but at the time, I thought I was just being nice or thoughtful. In fact, I probably was. To everybody except myself. For most of my youth, I was a codependent chameleon.

Then, I remember being a senior in college when a male friend of mine told me that he loved bumping into me because he never knew what I would be wearing. I was still a chameleon because I was always changing what I wore, but there was a difference. My outfits were now an expression of who I was on the inside, not who I was trying to be for someone else. In college, I embraced all aspects of my character and personality, and I expressed them in what I wore. This meant that on some days I'd be dressed in sweater sets with pearls, and other days I'd have a miniskirt on with platform shoes and a black string choker. You could also find me in jeans and "hippie" shirts, long maxi dresses, all in black, or all in sweatpants and fleeces. I dressed based on my mood, and I loved it all. There were very few styles of clothing that I avoided, and regardless of what I was wearing, I felt like I was standing in my boots and being true to myself. (Minus that one time when I thought I could lean into the goth look.)

Unfortunately, after college I had mostly decided on a pretty neutral "middle-of-the-road" wardrobe. It was easier to comply with external social expectations that way. Between the ages of 22 and 27 (when I got married), something shifted inside me that re-activated my latent tendency to be a more codependent. My focus on conforming—instead of personal expression—became increasingly detrimental. Over the course of the subsequent 12 years of marriage, I lost touch with who I was... who I am inside. I lost myself entirely and had to claw my way back to knowing myself, and it all started with an introduction. I greeted myself in the same way you "meet and greet" other people.

I identified who I was, what I did, and what I wanted to do and be. Not in relation to other people, but as myself alone. We don't do that in our lives, especially as women. When we meet someone and they ask us about ourselves, our go-to answer is to say who we are in relation to someone else:

I'm (blank's) mother.

I'm so-and-so's daughter.

I'm his/her spouse.

When you hear men introduce themselves, more often than not, they just state their name. Or their name and their work title or job. Why do we, as women, not do this? I think there are two reasons: 1) We have been trained that way, and 2) connection is inherent to our nature, so stating how we are connected to others may feel more natural than simply stating our name.

I still giggle in my head every time I formally introduce myself or someone else. My mind always flashes back to the scene from the *Bridget Jones' Diary* movie in which Bridget (Renée Zellwegger) is introducing Mark (Colin Firth) to her work colleague[3]:

Bridget: (thinking) *Ah, introduce people with thoughtful details.* To Perpetua: "Perpetua, This is Mark Darcy. Mark's a prematurely middle-aged prick with a cruel-raced[4] ex-wife." To Mark: "Perpetua is a flat-assed old bag who spends her time bossing me around."

If you read any of the comments on the YouTube clip of that scene, the basic consensus is that this gets filed under: *Things you wish you*

---

3 All script text is the property and copyright of its respective authors, artists, and labels.
4 Yes, that's what it said. I had to turn captions on to verify it and watch a few times. Yikes!

*could say but can't.* But what if we could? What would we say? (Obviously, not the racist and rude bits, though.)

More importantly, what would you say about yourself? How would you introduce yourself if you didn't feel you had to control or censor what you were saying? How would you like to be introduced by others? And now here's the PhD-level question:

What if you could create your greeting... What if you could *create yourself?*

Well, you can! That's what this entire book has been about, babe! 50 is just a number, a moment in time. It could be 40, or 30, or 60, or 70. It's a line in the sand. It's a point in time that marks a moment. Your moment... or not. Only you can choose when you want to embrace the Fuck It! Life. Nobody can tell you to do it. I can't. Your mother can't. Your therapist can't. Your spouse can't. Only you can. It's up to you.

For me, 50 has been my point in time. My moment. It's the point at which I decided that I simply didn't want to do things the way they've always been done. The moment in which I decided I both wanted and was *allowed* to have a say in how I was living my life—the moment in which I decided to fully *claim* my life as my own.

Now, let's be honest for a second. While 50 was the line in the sand for me, it's always been about both progress and the process. I've been greeting and creating myself for years now. It wasn't a gestalt shift that suddenly happened when I woke up on my 50th birthday to cake and presents. This has been a gradual unfolding that was a result of all that came before it. When the "a-ha!" moment happened, it all came together into one simple motto: "50 and Fuck It!" (Thank you, Mr. Troll-Man.) Yes, "thank you" because gratitude is both freeing and life-changing. Though, I do have one suggestion... If you don't like something: Scroll, don't troll. It really is that easy, my friends. Scrolling is a choice, just like trolling is. You don't need to respond to everything. So for everyone's sake ... scroll, don't troll. You'll be happier, and maybe the world will start to be kinder.

When you know yourself and understand what is balanced for you—when you're willing to create yourself—Fuck It! freedom is yours to embrace. Without apology, qualifiers, or explanation. And, frankly, if not at 50... when?

So bring it on! Grab your life by the horns and say, "This is who I am!" Then say Fuck It! to all the rest. You've earned it, and you deserve it.

# Fuck It! You're 50 (or 40, or 30...)

In short, the actual age doesn't matter. While I came to this conclusion around 50, you can reap the benefits of the Fuck It! Lifestyle at any age.

There's so much power in standing in your boots, but it's a power that isn't like anything we see portrayed on TV, in the news, or in movies. It's a power that is calm, grounded, and healthy. It's not a power that imposes on others, but one that strives to live in harmony with others while maintaining your presence. It's a power that is not apologetic. It doesn't require you to explain, justify, rationalize, or generalize.

Fuck It! power is also self-sustaining. When you are in your power, you don't need to rely on others to fuel you. In fact, Fuck It! power has nothing to do with the outside world. It's your own little internal generator, if you will. It doesn't need approval, validation, agreement, or acceptance from anyone but you.

This does not mean that it's confrontational or aggressive and imposing. If your power requires you to convince others of something, it's not true power—nor is it the calm grounded power of Fuck It! When you are in your Fuck It! power, you live from a place that goes beyond the whims and personalities of the outside world. Of course, some may not like this version of you, and that's okay. Change always takes a period of adjustment. Others may simply be uncomfortable seeing someone own and claim their space on the planet. Again, that's about them. Fuck It! isn't about anyone else, just as it's not about imposing yourself on others. This is about you... you getting to truly live your life in a way that is aligned with who you are deep inside, not who somebody told you to be.

While Fuck It! has a proclamation, it's actually a reclamation. It's a reclaiming of who you are deep inside... who you were before life and all the externalized stuff got at you and molded a different version of you in order to fit in or play along. Before life told you to be someone else, or at least that you should try to be someone else.

You know this person. You know you.

For some of us we haven't seen that person for many decades, maybe since we were 5 or 9 years old. For others, you may last remember being yourself in college or your 20s, after you got through the trying teen years. It doesn't matter how old you were when you last felt free to be yourself; It matters that you remember that authentic version of yourself and call it forth now to help you reclaim your voice and your inner power.

Fuck It! is the first step toward reacquainting yourself with... you. It's a tool that allows you to say no, just as it encourages you to say yes. It's the first step to standing in your boots and truly living.

# (Author's Note)

"50 and Fuck It!" started out as an internal joke of sorts. I kept it to myself and giggled in my own head every time I heard myself saying it in my thoughts. You might need to, too. It's like trying on a pair of shoes. Sometimes you need to wear them a bit in your home to get comfortable with them before wearing them outside.

After I had been saying it to myself for a few weeks, I shared it with my friend Patty. I mentioned her in Chapter 9. In some ways, I was taking it for a test drive. While I knew it was powerful (and funny) for me, I didn't know how it would land with other people. So I did what I normally do, and I tested it out. The result? It landed well. (I believe her exact words were: "I love that!" especially after I explained its genesis.) From there, I shared it with another friend who called me on the morning of my birthday. Ali had a similar reaction to Patty, and that was enough for me to publicly embrace the "50 and Fuck It!" sentiment. It wasn't until a few nights later that I realized it really had legs, which prompted me to write this book!

As a birthday surprise, my friend Sally arranged a Zoom meeting with several of our friends from high school. We're all turning 50 this year, or have recently, and so we had a good time chatting about life and this milestone event we would all be experiencing. I shared the new motto with them on the call, and it was met with laughter, smiles, support, and what I'd call a good amount of empowerment. As an energy worker, I could sense the shift in everybody on the call as they briefly contemplated using it in their own life. Suddenly, life seemed more possible, more vibrant, and a heck of a lot more fun!

Who could ask for more, to be honest?

To imagine a second act in life with more vibrancy, more hope, more joy, more love, and more fun was nothing I could have expected when I was younger. Remember, I thought 50 was old! And now I see 50 as the start of something magical. I see 50 as the beginning of anything and everything my heart desires.

My hope is that you can embrace this potential, too. Whether you're 50 or any other age, it's never too late—or too early—to embrace the tenets of the Fuck It! Lifestyle. You deserve a life that makes your heart smile. You deserve a life that brings you joy. Most of all, you deserve to live a life as who you are and who you want to be.

And if people in your life have trouble seeing it that way, just turn to them, smile, and then say: "Fuck It!" and do what is right for you anyway.

I have loved writing this book for you, for me, and for all our friends and loved ones. It has been an absolute blast! My hope is that it helps you as much as it has helped me. And if you're turning 50 when you read this: Happy Birthday!! xo

# Fuck It! Inspirational People I Love

There are many people in my personal life, or who have private social media accounts, who I find inspirational in the "Fuck It!" way. While I can't share their info, I thought it would be fun to share some of the *public* personas that I go to when my "Fuck It!" compass goes wonky and I've lost my way. It happens.

To follow is a list of people on Instagram who have inspired me, and at times validated me, through sharing their lives. I invite you to check them out yourself and let their authentic approach to life inspire you. Or find your own people who inspire you to say "Fuck It!" more often, and curate your own feed and share them with the rest of us. I've created the hashtag #50andFuckIt so we can all connect and share with each other. And yes, the following list is a bit Brit heavy. What can I say? I'm an Anglophile, and Fuck It! I like what I like:

- **Valerie Bertinelli (@wolfiesmom)**—Admittedly, I'm late to #teamvalerie, but I'm glad I got there eventually. Her authentic approach to life has been hard-earned, and it is an absolute pleasure to watch her gush over her son and live life on her terms.
- **Carla Birnberg (@carlabirnberg)**—In Chapter 1, I refer to Carla and her "unapologetically myself" motto. Carla has

been a friend for a few decades, having gone to college together (albeit a few years apart), and I always appreciate her very honest approach to life and relationships.

- **Dominique Davis (@itsgirldom)**—I stumbled onto Dominique Davis' original IG account (@allthatisthree, now @allthatisshe) and instantly fell in love with her creativity. Over time, I grew to really like the woman behind the brand, so I followed her solo account (among their other accounts—like I said, they're very creative!). She is a woman who shares her joy, her frustrations, and her humanity in really endearing ways. Plus, she's genuinely really kind, and their dog, Elvis, is adorable!

- **Austyn Farrell (@austyn_farrell)**—Austyn lives his life out loud and is one of the funniest people ever. He (and his videos) single-handedly got me through some of the worst days of lockdown, and I continue to tell people about him and send his videos to friends who need a pick-me-up. More importantly, though, Austyn is real. He shares the ups and the downs of his life, and I find myself rooting for him time and time again. He's also genuinely kind.

- **Charlotte-Anne Fidler (@charlotte_annefidler)**—The views of her home are one of the best visual escapes, and she's just genuinely lovely to chat with. Plus, like so many other women, she has reinvented herself and created a 2nd act for her life that is amazing.

- **Jen Louden (@jenlouden)**—Admittedly, another person I'm a bit late to the party on, but 100% here for the messages she shares for both women and writers. Jen is a writer's writer, and a champion of other people's work. She is authentic, fun, knowledgeable, and living her best life at 60. Plus, she's a dog lover. If you want to feel inspired to go after your dreams, follow Jen!

- **Julie Montagu (@juliemontagu)**—Julie is an American who married into the British aristocracy. A good friend of mine suggested I follow her, and I'm so glad she did. Across several accounts, Julie shares glimpses into her life in ways that I find both motivating and aspirational. Most importantly, though, Julie feels very real and shows up exactly as she is, whether she's ripping up carpet, cold swimming, or about to be on TV as a royal correspondent. She may be a Viscountess, but she's also just Julie, all the time, and it's really lovely.

- **Pinky Patel (@pinkypatel)**—Pinky is a comedian who found her calling producing viral videos on life, mostly from an authentic female perspective. She brilliantly addresses social issues while also making us laugh. Her fan base is predominantly female (with a love for sparkly crowns!), and I have found her to be someone whose voice I look forward to hearing on a regular basis.

- **Shonda Rhimes (@shondarhimes)**—Again, another person I was late to follow, but once I did, I was glad I had found her. Though she's not as active as the others on this list, I couldn't leave her out. Her calm and quiet approach to sharing her life (and earned wisdom) is leadership through modeling what's possible if/when you show up for yourself.

- **Katie Sturino (@katiesturino)**—Katie is the author and founder of Megababe, a beauty company. Additionally, she is a body-positive blogger who never apologizes for living her life exactly as she is. She also offers us loving reminders that buying into the "better or worse" script is designed to keep people down.

- **Paula Sutton (@hillhousevintage)**—Paula is a self-described "accidental influencer" who is both authentic and talented.

Furthermore, she is one of the most thoughtful and kind people I've had the pleasure of getting to know online. She is 100% the real deal, and her joy comes through in everything she does. She gives 50+ a totally new perspective and shares her beautiful home, life, and country aesthetic to her half-a-million+ followers, inspiring others to create a life that they love. I have loved getting to know her and watching her soar over the last few years. You will, too!

- **Jordan Syatt (@syattfitness)**—Jordan doesn't mince his words and cares passionately about helping others through what he shares. He also doesn't do paid advertising on anything he, himself, uses and recommends. Hence, I hesitate to call him an "influencer", but he's definitely influenced me—in all the right ways. Plus he's hella funny!

- **Georgia Tennant (@georgiatennantofficial)**—One of the funnier people I've followed on Instagram, Georgia has a way of sharing her life in her stories that is both curated and real. It always leaves me with a sense of "what you see is what you get" combined with a teensy glimpse inside her thoughts, which ultimately is both very validating and entertaining. Of course, it helps that I'm a big fan of dry wit and humour.

- **Derek Warburton (@derekwarburton)**—Derek is a dear friend of mine and someone who inspires me regularly with his "all-in" approach to life. He is a man who has embraced all of himself, including his less-than-awesome younger days, to flourish today. His love for all things style may seem over the top to some, but it's grounded in a truly humble and grateful human being.

In addition to the above accounts, here is a short list of a few more people that I find myself seeking out on a regular basis. They are all different in the type of content they share, though each one does so in a meaningful and authentic way... yes, even when they're using their platform for work.

- **Barlow and Bear (@barlowandbear)**—These two power-house women won a grammy for writing and producing their own music... on social media! You go, girls!

- **Irene (@irenemylife)**—Whenever I need a dose of English country life, women supporting women, or a reminder on how we can choose to live differently (she's plant-based) and create our own paths, I visit Irene's page for inspiration.

- **Charlotte Jacklin (@charlottejacklin)**—Her dreamy posts and her body-positive commentary are a welcome balm in a noisy landscape.

- **Kunal Nayyar (@buddhas.in.jeans)**—Kunal has an account in his own name, but I genuinely love this second account he created.

- **Alicia Mccarvell (@aliciamccarvell)**—Funny, irreverent, thoughtful, and 100% human, Alicia shares her life with us as a body-positive influencer.

- **Slim Sherri (@therealslimsherri)**—If you're a member of GenX, you need to follow Sherri for her hilarious (and relatable) videos.

Finally, let's have fun online! I thought it would be fun for us to share our stories with each other, so I've created the hashtag #50andFuckIt. This will help us find each other and share in the joy of reclaiming our lives at 50—or at least laughing about the more humorous aspects of the process. I can't be the only one who talks about farting after a colonoscopy, now can I? See you out there!

# Acknowledgments

I'd like to start by thanking the beautiful women who shared their time and read an advanced copy of the book to give me feedback. Writing a book with "F*ck" in the title felt a little bit daunting, to be honest. Ali, Jen, Katy, Liz, Muna, Sally, and Sarah—you quelled my fears about using "fuck" and validated my words. You also helped make the book better and have inspired me to expand beyond this single book into other offerings to help more people. Thank you, from my heart. Cheers, dears!

Another big thank you goes out to some incredibly supportive people who were cheering me on as I wrote this book and after it was finished. Alex, Andy, Franny, John, Paul, and Teri—thank you for always being honest while also being the best cheerleaders a woman could ask for.

Thank you also to my talented book team: Lisa, Winter, Natalie, Michelle and Joe, and Myra, who helped me bring my vision for this work to life (along with the fun companion pieces we have created!) and for keeping me focused when I wanted to wander a bit or got a little stubborn. It happens. ; )

To my friends far and wide, both in real life and online: When I see you showing up in life, I smile. Thank you for sharing your life with the rest of us and for being you, even when it hasn't always been easy. You are all amazing human beings.

Finally, a big thank you to my mom. Though swearing wasn't necessarily condoned in our house, you showed me that it's okay to say "fuck it" and step away when things aren't going right and life has gotten frustrating. While it didn't carry exactly the same intent that I convey in this book, it was most certainly a place to start. Thank you for always being supportive and for being a great travel companion and friend. I love you.

*Thank you, all.*

*xoxo,*

*me*

# About the Author

*"I write from my soul to understand my humanity...*
*which hopefully then helps others to better understand theirs."*
Martina E. Faulkner

Martina E. Faulkner, LMSW is a pioneer in wholeself wellness focusing on connection—connection to self, to others, and to something greater. As a new thought leader and author, she explores the relationship between our core divinity and our vibrant humanity, often using her own personal stories as the vehicle. Martina's writing is infused with elements from her experience as a certified life coach, licensed therapist, intuitive psychic-medium, and Reiki Master Teacher. She is the author of five books across the genres of self-help, poetry, and children's, with more on the way—including two novels. Her debut children's book, *When the World Went Quiet,* was written in response to the Covid-19 pandemic to give children something positive to focus on during difficult times and has been endorsed by world-renowned conservationists.

In 2019, Martina started Inspirebytes Omni Media (IOM), an independent publishing company that focuses on supporting authors and artists by changing the approach to publishing, making it more collaborative, equitable, and transparent while giving voice to talented individuals from around the world.

**Join Martina on Instagram and Facebook (@martinaefaulkner),**
**or to learn more, visit: MartinaFaulkner.com and Inspirebytes.com.**

# More by the Author

*50 and F\*ck It! Companion Self-Guided Workbook*
(Coming early 2023)
*Who Are You? The 365-Day 5-Year Journal to Know Yourself Better*
(Coming early 2023)
*What if..?: How to Create the Life You Want Using the Power of Possibility*
*Infinite In My Heart: Poems of Love, Loss, and Hope*
*Crafting the Perfect College Essay: Write Your Best Essay in 3 Easy Steps*
*Crafting the Perfect College Essay: The Workbook*

❧ ❧ ❧

**Children's Books by the Author as Tia Martina**

*When the World Went Quiet*
*Princess Wigglebottom and the Forgotten Christmas*

❧ ❧ ❧

**Martina E. Faulkner is a contributing author for the following books**

*365 Moments of Grace*
*365 Life Shifts*
*365 Soulful Messages*

❧ ❧ ❧

All of these books are responsibly printed using print-on-demand technology, in order to minimize our impact on the planet and the environment. Learn more at: www.inspirebytes.com/why-we-publish-differently/

## Finally, if you received
## this book as a birthday gift ...

# Happy Birthday!

Made in the USA
Monee, IL
18 February 2023

28154040R00073